W9-AHO-880

A Portrait of Wittgenstein as a Young Man

A PORTRAIT OF WITTGENSTEIN AS A YOUNG MAN

Edited by
G. H. von Wright

With an Introduction by Anne Keynes

From the Diary of David Hume Pinsent 1912-1914

Basil Blackwell

First published 1990

Basil Blackwell Ltd
108 Cowley Road, Oxford, OX4 1JF, UK

Basil Blackwell, Inc.
3 Cambridge Center
Cambridge, Massachusetts 02142, USA

British Library Cataloguing in Publication Data

A CIP catalogue record for this book is available from the British Library.

Library of Congress Cataloging in Publication Data

Pinsent, David Hume, 1891–1918.
A portrait of Wittgenstein as a young man: from the diary of David Hume Pinsent 1912–1914/edited by G. H. von Wright: with an introduction by Anne Pinsent Keynes.
p. cm.
ISBN 0-631-17511-3
1. Wittgenstein, Ludwig, 1889–1951. 2. Philosophers – Great Britain – Biography, 3. Pinsent, David Hume, 1891–1918 – Diaries.
I. Wright, G. H. von (Georg Henrik), 1916– . II. Title.
B3376.W564P49 1990
192 – dc20 89-49598
CIP

Typeset in Monotype Lasercomp 11½ on 13pt
by Graphicraft Typesetters Limited, Hong Kong
Printed in Great Britain by Billing & Sons Ltd, Worcester

Contents

Foreword

Wittgenstein came to Cambridge in the Michaelmas Term of 1911 to attend Russell's lectures. He was then still officially registered in the department of engineering at Manchester. By the Lent Term of 1912 he had become an advanced student (later called 'research student') at Cambridge and a member of Trinity College.

David Pinsent's first meeting with Wittgenstein took place, to the best of our knowledge, in February, at one of the weekly evening meetings, known as 'squashes', which Russell held in his rooms at Trinity. In the diary entry for 1 February, Pinsent records having met there 'a young German attending Russell's lectures'. The 'German' made a distinct impression. The diary says that he 'was very amusing unconsciously, and told a number of preposterous grim stories of murders with a wonderful serious indignation and fervour!'

In an entry four weeks later (29 February), we are told that at another meeting in Russell's rooms there was among the guests 'a German individual – undergraduate – a pleasant person, over here to take exercise!' We do not know for sure whether the references are to the same 'German' individual or to two different ones. But there is every reason to think that at least one, if not both, allude to the 'German' Pinsent met with Russell on 4 May and whom, in the entry for that day, he calls 'Vittgenstein'.

Pinsent continued to mis-spell the name until the two friends set out on their tour to Iceland in September. Yet in the intervening months they were to pass a considerable amount of time in each other's company. They attended concerts together – both being highly musical – and Pinsent, indeed, served as a 'subject' in the experimental work on rhythm in music which Wittgenstein was then undertaking in the Psychological Laboratory, recently founded by Charles Samuel Myers, at Cambridge.

Already, at the end of May, Wittgenstein proposed to Pinsent that they should go to Iceland together before the beginning of the next Michaelmas term. They set out on the expedition on 5 September, and returned to England on 3 October.

Both were at Cambridge for the entire academic year 1912–13. There seem to have been no plans for a new journey together until the middle of the Long Vacation when Wittgenstein, then in Austria, announced that he would come to England in August 'to go to Spain' with Pinsent. When he arrived, he had three different suggestions: to go to Andorra, or the Azores, or Norway. They decided on the third alternative, and the journey took place between 29 August and 1 October. Some ten days later Wittgenstein returned to Norway alone. Before doing so, he visited Pinsent in his parents' home in Birmingham. Pinsent saw him off at the railway station early on the morning of 8 October. This was the last time the two friends saw each other.

Wittgenstein stayed in Norway for the whole academic year 1913–14 – with a short interruption at Christmas when he went home to Vienna. The germination of the thoughts which eventually crystallized in the *Tractatus* was now in full progress. After his return from Norway to Austria in June 1914 a third journey with Pinsent was planned for later in the summer. Andorra was again mentioned as a possible destination. But with the outbreak of war none of this could be. On 7 August Wittgenstein enlisted as a volunteer gunner in the Austro-Hungarian cause. He would remain a soldier for the duration.

During the first years of the war the friends corresponded. No letters from Wittgenstein to Pinsent are known to survive. (See however below p. 101.) But more than ten letters from Pinsent to Wittgenstein came to light in Austria in 1988. They are here reproduced with the kind permission of Frau Charlotte Eder of Vienna. The last three letters, from 1916, are in German and I have here re-translated them into English.

David Pinsent was killed in an aeroplane accident at the Royal Aircraft Establishment, Farnborough, in May 1918. Wittgenstein first learned of his friend's death in a letter from Pinsent's mother. This letter and two others from Ellen Pinsent were among those recently found in Austria. They too are printed here – together with two letters from Wittgenstein to Mrs Pinsent.

Wittgenstein's *Tractatus logico-philosophicus* is dedicated to the memory of David H. Pinsent.

Not long after Wittgenstein's death in 1951, Lady Adrian, *née* Hester Pinsent, showed to a number of his friends extracts she had made from the diary of her brother, David Pinsent, relating to his friendship with Wittgenstein. It struck us all how 'true to life' these passages were in the picture they gave of Wittgenstein, not only as a young man, but also as the man whom my contemporaries and I had known in the 1930s and 1940s.

The question of publishing the extracts was raised at the time but left pending. Much later, in 1988, a query from Mikael Karlsson, professor of philosophy in the University of Reykjavik, caused me to re-read the extracts. Again I was struck by the freshness and truthfulness of the impression they convey. A little later I heard about the discovery of the Pinsent letters in Austria. Thus I was prompted to raise the question of publication again with David Pinsent's nephew and nieces, the second Lord Adrian and his sisters Mrs Jennet Campbell and Mrs Anne Keynes. They agreed to my suggestion and kindly entrusted me with the task of editing the relevant parts of the diary for publication. In this task I have been generously assisted by Mrs Keynes who also kindly agreed to write an introductory account of David Hume Pinsent and his family background. She and her cousin Sir Christopher Pinsent have helped to identify those persons mentioned but not fully identified in the diary. I am further indebted to Mr Sveinn Eldon and Dr Simon Keynes for assistance with checking the Icelandic place-names. The map showing Pinsent's and Wittgenstein's travel route in Iceland is based on an original by Dr Keynes.

All entries in the diary which make reference to Wittgenstein are printed here. A few passages, indicated by ellipses . . ., have been omitted as irrelevant to Pinsent's acquaintance with Wittgenstein. Orthographical mistakes and mistakes in the spelling of place names have been silently corrected but otherwise interference with the spontaneous and sometimes laconic style of the diary has been kept to a minimum. An effort has been made to standardize punctuation in connection with abbreviations, notably for ante- and post-meridian. Substantive interventions are enclosed in square brackets. Footnotes marked by arabic numerals are by the editor. All other footnotes are David Pinsent's. The editing of the letters follows the principles adopted in the volume of correspondence, *Briefe* (Frankfurt: Suhrkamp Verlag, 1980), edited by B. F. McGuinness and G. H. von Wright.

For a full account of Wittgenstein in Cambridge before the 1914–1918 war the reader is referred to Brian McGuinness's admirable biography *Wittgenstein, A Life: Young Ludwig (1889–1921)* (London: Gerald Duckworth & Co. Ltd, 1988).

Georg Henrik von Wright
Cambridge 1989

Introduction

David Hume Pinsent, born 24 May 1891, was the eldest of the three children of Hume Chancellor Pinsent, a Birmingham solicitor, and his wife Ellen Frances, *née* Parker.

Pinsents had been yeomen farmers in Devon, but Hume Pinsent's maternal great-grandfather was a nephew of David Hume the philosopher, and he and his brothers were sent to the Edinburgh Academy and Amersham Hall, Reading, a dissenting academy for Nonconformists, and a recognized route to the universities and professions.

Parkers were originally royal park-keepers, and later minor landowners in Lancashire. Ellen Parker liked to recall that her maternal ancestors included one of the so-called Lancashire witches from the Forest of Bowland, and a sea-captain who sailed for New England in 1649, bought a share of the island of Nantucket, and was always said to have been able to provide a crew for his ship from his illegitimate sons. Her father, an evangelical clergyman in Claxby, Lincolnshire, had thirteen children of whom she was the youngest. Educated at home by her sisters and governesses, she was influenced largely by her older brother Robert, who rebelled against his father and became an unorthodox free-thinker at Eton, and King's College, Cambridge. Here he met Karl

Pearson, later to become head of the Galton Eugenics Laboratory at University College, London, and invited him home to Claxby. Ellen Parker rapidly absorbed the unorthodox views of Pearson and her brother and later joined Pearson's Men's and Women's Club where she met Hume Pinsent, from St John's College, Cambridge, then reading for the Bar with Robert Parker.

Hume Pinsent married Ellen Parker in 1888 and went to live in Birmingham, to join the firm of solicitors, Pinsent and Co., founded by his older brother, later Sir Richard Pinsent, a president of the Law Society. Interested in literature, music and education, he read widely, involved himself in various educational institutions as well as his brother's firm, and eventually became a member of the Council of Birmingham University, and its treasurer. According to his son, he retired just in time to avoid being made vice-chancellor, and moved in 1913 to Foxcombe Hill, near Oxford, to read his large collection of books.

Ellen Pinsent, in spite of her lack of formal education, published four novels in her early married days. These reflect her country rectory upbringing and her interest in contemporary social problems: *Jenny's Case*, still readable in spite of an excess of Lincolnshire dialect, a contemporary literary fashion, described the all too common case of the abandoned unmarried mother; *No Place for Repentance* concerned an alcoholic curate, and *Job Hildred* a mentally disturbed artist. As her children grew up she turned from fiction to real life. She chose for her presidential address to the Birmingham Ladies' Literary and Debating Society to speak on 'Training the Mentally Deficient', and shocked her listeners with the problems she revealed. Unlike them, she had visited the Girls' Night Shelter and the Home for Fallen Women. Soon she was secretary of the local branch of the Society for the Prevention of Cruelty to Children, and then chairman of Birmingham's Special Schools sub-committee. In 1904 she was appointed, as the only woman member, to the Royal Commission on the Care and Control of the Feeble-Minded, and visited the United States in the following year to inspect lunatic asylums and colonies for the mentally deficient. On her return she campaigned, to a certain extent under the influence of Karl Pearson and the Eugenics Movement, vigorously to improve conditions for the mentally disabled in the United Kingdom. In 1911 she was the first woman to be elected to Birmingham City Council, and in 1913 she was rewarded for her enthusiasm and persistence with the passing of the Mental Deficiency Act. This established the Board of Control, responsible for the care and control of the mentally deficient, to which she was appointed an honorary commissioner.

Meanwhile David Pinsent and his brother Richard, and sister Hester, were brought up in Harborne, Birmingham, near their cousins in Selly Oak, in a close and comfortable family atmosphere. If Ellen Pinsent was often out visiting schools, inspecting mental institutions, and attending committees, she nevertheless found time to organize dinner parties for friends and parties for the young in the billiard room. She played tennis with her sons and explored the countryside in the family's first motorcar. In the evenings Hume Pinsent played billiards, took his sons to concerts and most of all enjoyed reading to them aloud. There were frequent family gatherings and visits to and from relatives, particularly Maisie and Evelyn Radford, daughters of Hume Pinsent's sister Edith. Amateur musicians, who encouraged David Pinsent's piano playing, they were to produce between the wars, a number of operas, including the first English performances of Mozart's 'La clemenza di Tito' in 1930, and 'Idomeneo' in 1937, at Falmouth in Cornwall.

The boys were educated at Marlborough College, and for many years their summer holidays from school were spent in Castle Townshend, County Cork, Ireland, the childhood home of Ellen Pinsent's friend and colleague on the Special Schools sub-committee, Dr Violet Coghill. She was a member of the large Anglo-Irish family of Somervilles, Penroses and Coghills which included Edith Somerville, co-author of the Irish RM stories with another cousin Martin Ross, and Nevill Coghill, much later Professor of English Literature at Oxford. Dr Coghill's brother, Sir Egerton, an enthusiastic sailor, organized regattas in the harbour for family and visitors. There were picnics, tennis parties, charades and concerts. David and Richard Pinsent took part in all of these, David particularly enjoying the sailing races and concerts. Later, when the boys had left school, there were individual visits to France, Germany and Switzerland, to learn French and German, and for short walking tours in the mountains. The last family holiday of all was in Switzerland in the winter of 1913–14 to learn to ski.

David Pinsent went up to Trinity College, Cambridge, in 1910 with a scholarship in mathematics, Richard Pinsent to Balliol College, Oxford, in 1913 with an exhibition in Natural Sciences.

At Cambridge David Pinsent joined the University Music Club, the Union, the Eugenics Society, and, briefly, the Fabian Society. He was interested in philosophy, regularly attended Bertrand Russell's squashes and meetings of the Cambridge Heretics Society, and he helped to found a short-lived society, the 'Sophists'. J. M. Keynes, whose father had been at Amersham Hall with Hume Pinsent, and who was recruiting for the semi-secret Conversazione Society, or Apostles, is known to have considered David Pinsent as an 'embryo', or candidate for membership of the Society, but in the event he was not elected. (Wittgenstein, a reluctant Apostle, was elected in November 1912.) He made many friends among his contemporaries, including George Thomson, a future Nobel laureate in physics, and of course Wittgenstein. In winter he went riding and skating, in summer he played tennis. He continued his piano studies (Beethoven and Schubert sonatas, Bach preludes and fugues), went to a great many concerts in Cambridge, and as many as he could in London, on his own, or with his Radford cousins, hearing Beethoven and Brahms symphonies for the first time, and developing a particular passion for Beethoven. He worked reasonably hard at mathematics, and emerged from his final examinations as a Senior Wrangler, with a first class degree.

In 1962 Sir George Thomson, Master of Corpus Christi College, Cambridge, wrote in autobiographical notes for his family: 'David was the most brilliant man of my year, among the most brilliant I have ever met. Rather quaint in appearance, being slight in build and with a very large head, he yet had a remarkable charm and made friends easily, not only with intellectual people. He was my closest friend at Trinity and we used to go for walks together. He was by way of being a pure mathematician with a leaning to philosophy, and was a friend of Wittgenstein. They went on a trip to Iceland together one Long Vacation, and on another occasion to Norway. He opened my eyes to some of the possibilities of philosophy, on which till then I had held the naivest ideas. He had an aversion from what he called plumbing, by which he meant anything practical which did not interest him. However he was readily interested and the realm of plumbing diminished rather quickly . . .'*

When war broke out in 1914 Richard Pinsent, who had spent one year at Balliol, immediately volunteered, and obtained a commission in Kitchener's Army as a second lieutenant in the Royal Warwickshire Regiment. After training in England, he went out to France with his regiment in June 1915, and was killed in the trenches in October. His cousin Philip had been killed a few weeks earlier in an air flight over the German lines. David Pinsent, who had spent a year studying law in Birmingham, reading for the Bar after leaving Cambridge, had failed to get a commission at the outbreak of war owing to his slight physique. He had moved to London to work for his uncle Robert, now Lord Parker of Waddington and a High Court Judge, and to take his law examinations. But soon after Richad Pinsent's departure for France, he joined the Ministry of Munitions to increase the output of machine guns for the Front. After his brother's death, and that of another cousin, he tried again for a commission in the army and failing that to volunteer as a private soldier. Refused a second time, he trained as a tool-

* Quoted by kind permission of Sir John Thomson, GCMG.

setter in a Birmingham munitions factory, and in March 1916 was sent to the RAF Factory at Farnborough where he spent the next eight months working extremely hard with very little leave, 'clad in excessively greasy blue overalls bathed all over in lard oil'. 'We are making the fork universal joints which go onto the end of the RAF special aeroplane stream-line wire ...' he wrote to his parents. 'We are in the proud position of making joints for the whole of the British Aeroplane Industry, we being Murray and myself and three people on the night shift.' In fact, although it was exhausting work, he appreciated the experience, and developed considerable respect for his fellow workmen. 'Plumbing' was more rewarding than he would have guessed in his Cambridge days.

Meanwhile George Thomson and other Cambridge contemporaries were engaged on research in aerodynamics at Farnborough, and in the end persuaded David Pinsent to join them and use his mathematical rather than his manual skills for the war effort. At once he realized that this was the work for which he was really suited, and before long he experienced the tremendous excitement of flying for the first time. There were even occasional free weekends of which he took advantage to become engaged to a naval commander's daughter in Oxford. The engagement, though, fell victim to the impossibility of maintaining, let alone developing a relationship in wartime, and in fact his enthusiasm and energy were entirely concentrated on his experiments, which involved an increasing amount of flying in the primitive aeroplanes of the day. Ironically, his slight build was now an advantage in the small space available for a scientific observer, and he was soon busy preparing reports for the National Physical Laboratory on the results of his experiments. To his unscientific parents he wrote, 'The experiments show quite clearly how a compass behaves badly, and I think my work makes it clear why it does so, and thus how it can be made to behave better.' He lived with a group of scientists and mathematicians mostly from Cambridge, which included at various times the Nobellaureates-to-be F. W. Aston and G. P. Thomson, G. I. Taylor (later Sir Geoffrey Taylor, OM), F. A. Lindemann (later Lord Cherwell) and E. D. Adrian (later Lord Adrian, OM) who was working nearby as a doctor on shell shock at the Connaught Military Hospital, Aldershot.

By 1918 experiments needed experienced pilots prepared to take considerable aerobatic risks. In the spring David Pinsent's letters home described exploits which must have alarmed his parents, for he wrote 'I quite agree that the stunting is a bit exaggerated, but you must realize that this is only typical of the sort of thing they have to encourage in the Flying Corps. That sort of devil-may-care spirit is absolutely essential . . . There are a lot of experiments we've only recently been able to do because the old pilots refused to do them – said they were too dangerous . . . We've had if anything fewer accidents with these new men than we had with the old lot. Please don't worry. It really is absurdly safe, and I sometimes wish it wasn't quite so safe and then I might feel I was sharing some of the risks of these days.' Next week, 'It is so pleasant to be able to go out after tea again. When summertime comes it will be light up to 7.30 at least, and we shall begin flying in the evening.' He was killed on 8 May 1918.

David Pinsent kept 'an open and unselfconscious diary,' as Brian McGuinness describes it,* from his schooldays until the summer of 1914, faithfully recording his daily life. Sometimes he used it as a preliminary draft for his letters home, occasionally he commented on issues of the day such as Women's Suffrage and Home Rule for Ireland, more often he criticized books he had read or enthusiastically described concerts he had attended. The diary stops abruptly at the beginning of the war, and there are two long supplements written in December 1914 and 1915 from which the last entries are taken. He and Wittgenstein corresponded as best they could during the war, but never met again.

* McGuinness, p. 120.

After the war and the death of their two sons, Hume and Ellen Pinsent and their daughter Hester returned to Oxford from Birmingham, where Hume Pinsent had taken his nephews' place in Pinsent and Co. for the duration of the war. He died in 1920, and with Hester Pinsent now at Somerville College, Oxford, Ellen Pinsent moved to London to continue her work on mental welfare as a senior commissioner at the Board of Control.

In 1932, Ellen Pinsent retired to Boar's Hill, Oxford, with a CBE and an Honorary MA from Birmingham University. Still active, she wrote a report on the Oxford Mental Health Services, criticizing the quantity and quality of care available at that time. She was further rewarded for her achievements in 1937, when she became a Dame. When the Second World War began, she busied herself, now in her late seventies, with the local National Savings Group. Her home Rough Lee, named after that of Alice Nutter, the Lancashire Witch, was always a haven for visiting friends and relations, whether on leave from the forces, escaping from London air raids, resting after illness, or revising before examinations. She died there in 1949, and Gilbert Murray, OM, a neighbour on Boar's Hill, wrote to *The Times* to supplement her obituary: 'She was a friend and stimulus to rich and poor, learned and unlearned, to the children and to the "over-eighties", all could find in her house welcome and sympathy, help if needed and lively discussion of all subjects, grave and gay, with never a harsh note.'

David Pinsent's sister Hester, a schoolgirl in 1912, was a VAD nurse at the end of the 1914–18 war. She read history at Somerville college, Oxford, and in 1923 married E. D. Adrian, then a lecturer in physiology and Fellow (later Master) of Trinity College, Cambridge, whom she first met at David Pinsent's funeral in 1918. She continued her mother's work in mental health, and became a Dame herself in 1965. Wittgenstein used to call on her in Cambridge. According to Joan Bevan, whose husband was Wittgenstein's doctor, and in whose home he spent the last months of his life, these visits to David's sister were the only occasions on which he ever wore a tie. After Wittgenstein's death in 1951, Hester Adrian selected all the passages of interest in her brother's diaries that referred to Wittgenstein, and deposited them in the library of Trinity College. In her speech in 1965 at a farewell dinner for her husband's retirement as Master of Trinity she described her first visit to Trinity, in 1913: 'I came to see my brother David Pinsent take his degree, and incidentally was taken on the Cam in a canoe by Wittgenstein, probably a unique distinction!'

David Pinsent may well have found some of his other friends to be easier travelling companions than Wittgenstein; he certainly much enjoyed sailing and walking holidays with George Thomson and others, but he was well aware of Wittgenstein's singular quality, and wrote after what was to be their last meeting: 'Our acquaintance has been chaotic, but I have been very thankful for it. I am sure he has also.'

That Wittgenstein had is shown by the dedication of the *Tractatus*.

Anne Pinsent Keynes

List of Illustrations

The editor and publishers are especially grateful to Anne Keynes and to the Fellows and library staff of Trinity College, Cambridge, for providing the illustrations listed here.

Plates between pages 2 and 3

Extracts from

The Diary
of
David Pinsent
1912–1914

1 *Postcard from David Pinsent in Reykjavik to Hester Pinsent, 13 September 1912*

2 *Postcard from David Pinsent to his mother from Øistesø, Norway, 8 September 1913*

4.0 & rode on very fast for an hour to
an Inn just 50 Kilom: from Reykjavik,
where we put up for the night.* After about
half an hour's delay they shewed us our
rooms: and after changing I wrote this
diary. Supper was at 7.30. Afterwards
till 10.0 I read Wuthering Heights. Wittgenstein
was a bit sulky all the evening: he is
very sensitive if I get, momentarily,
a bit irritated over some trifle – as
I did tonight – I forget what about:
the result being that he was depressed &
silent for the rest of the evening. He is
always imploring me not to be irritable:
& I do my best, & really, I think, I have
not been so often this trip!

Sunday, September 22nd. It rained
& blew terribly all night. We had break-
-fast at 9.30. Then decided that, in any
case, we would go no further than
Chiterurente today, & that, as that is
only 4 hrs: ride, we would wait
till after lunch, to give the weather a

* It began to rain, & blew harder than ever
about 3.0, & we rode this hour right
through the storm.

3 *A page from David Pinsent's diary for 1912*

4 *David Pinsent at Glenfield, Foxcombe Hill, Oxford, in 1915*

5 *David Pinsent sailing in Falmouth Harbour, Cornwall, in 1916*

6 *Scientists at Chudleigh, Farnborough, in 1918, including: F. A. Lindemann, G. P. Thomson, W. S. Farren, F. W. Aston and David Pinsent*

7 *W. S. Farren, later director of the Royal Aircraft Establishment, Farnborough, and David Pinsent, aboard their plane in 1918*

8 *Dame Ellen Frances Pinsent,* née *Parker*

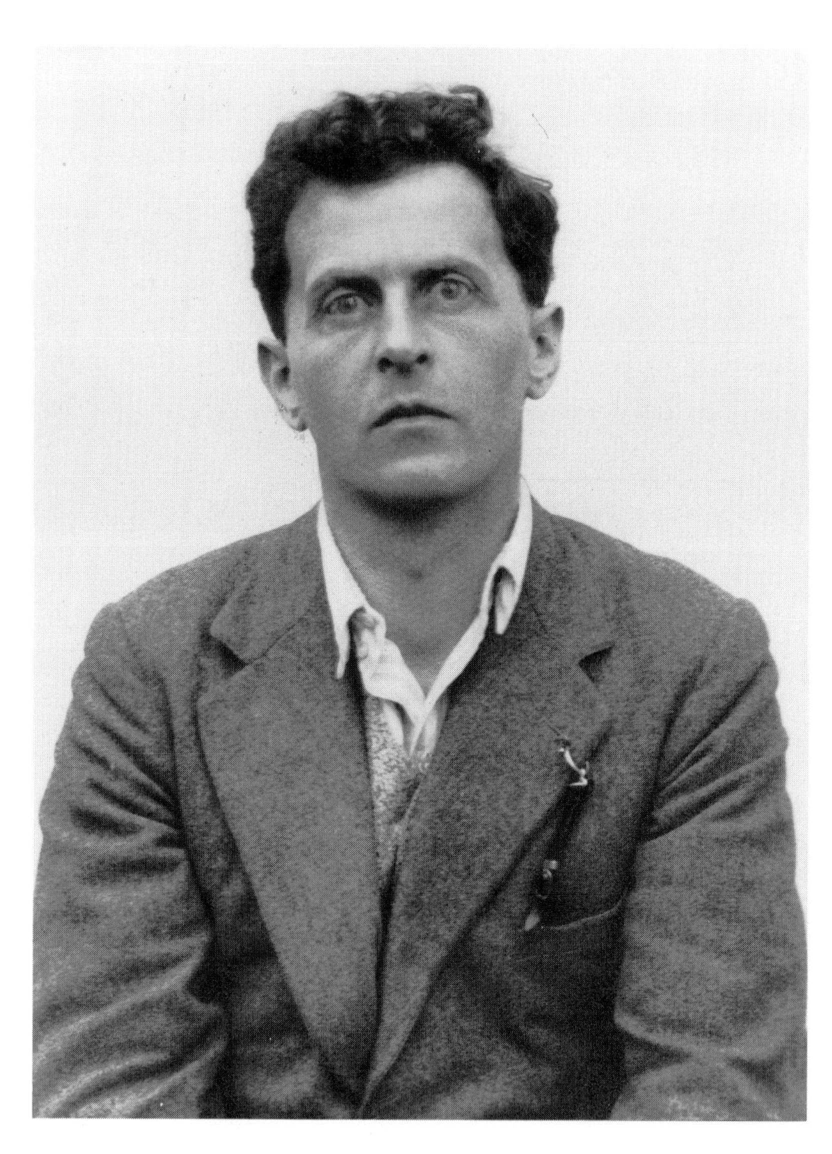

9 *Ludwig Wittgenstein*

1912

[*Saturday*] *May 4th, 1912*

At 5.0 I went to a concert, at the Guildhall – a chamber concert, including a very fine piano trio of Schubert's. I met Wittgenstein there – a German I have met before *chez* Russell – but he had to go early.

Monday, May 13th, 1912

At 2.30 I went *chez* Wittgenstein and we went on to the Psychological Laboratory, where I had arranged to act as a 'subject' in some experiments he is trying: to ascertain the extent and importance of rhythm in music. Not bad fun. Afterwards I had tea *chez lui*. He is quite interesting and pleasant, though his sense of humour is heavy.

Wednesday, May 15th, 1912

At 2.30 I went *chez* Wittgenstein, and we went on to the Psychological Laboratory for more experiments. Exactly as last time.

Saturday, May 18th, 1912

I went *chez* Wittgenstein. We went on to the Psychological Lab. and I underwent more experiments as before.[1] Afterwards I had tea *chez* Wittgenstein.

Tuesday, May 21st, 1912

At 2.0 I went *chez* Wittgenstein and on with him to the Psychological Laboratory. More experiments as usual.

Tuesday, May 28th, 1912

At 2.0 I went *chez* Wittgenstein and on to the Lab. for more experiments. That ended at 3.30.

Thursday, May 30th, 1912

At 11.0 pm I went *chez* Russell. There were lots there – including Békássy, Ogden and Wittgenstein and Crouschoff.[2] They mostly went at 11.30 but Wittgenstein and I stayed till 12.0. Wittgenstein was very amusing: he is reading philosophy up here, but has only just started systematic

[1] See the editor's Foreword, p. viii.

[2] The occasion was one of Russell's weekly evening 'squashes', in his rooms at Trinity. Ferenc Békássy (1893–1915), Hungarian aristocrat, educated at Bedales and at King's College, Cambridge, 1911–14, was an Apostle and an intimate friend of J. M. Keynes. He died in Bukovina (fighting in the same cause for which Wittgenstein himself enlisted) on 25 June 1915, a lieutenant in the 5th Honvéd Hussars. A posthumous collection of his verse *Adriatica and other Poems* was published in 1925, at Keynes's instigation, by the Hogarth Press. Charles Kay Ogden (1889–1957), linguistic psychologist, educated at Magdalene College, Cambridge, president 1911–24 of the Heretics Society, founder in 1912 of the *Cambridge Magazine*, and with F. P. Ramsey the original translator into English of Wittgenstein's *Logisch-Philosophische Abhandlung* – the *Tractatus Logico-Philosophicus*. Crouschoff remains unidentified.

reading: and he expresses the most naïve surprise that all the philosophers, he once worshipped in ignorance, are after all stupid and dishonest and make disgusting mistakes!

Friday, May 31st, 1912

At 3.0 I met Wittgenstein at the Psychological Lab., and had more rhythm-experiments. At the end he suddenly asked what I was doing during the vac. and proposed that I should come with him to Iceland. After my first surprise I asked what he estimated the cost would be: upon which he said – 'Oh, that doesn't matter: I have no money and you have no money – at least, if you have, it doesn't matter. But my father has a lot' – upon which he proposed that his father should pay for us both! I really don't know what to think: it would certainly be fun, and I could not afford it myself, and Wittgenstein seems very anxious for me to come. I deferred my decision and wrote home for advice: Iceland seems rather attractive: I gather that all inland travelling has to be done on horse back, which would be supreme fun! The whole idea attracts and surprises me: I have known Wittgenstein only for three weeks or so – but we seem to get on well together: he is very musical with the same tastes as I. He is an Austrian – but speaks English fluently. I should say about my age.

Saturday, June 1st, 1912

Went to the CUMC.[3] at 7.30 and strummed till 8.0. The usual concert began at 8.15. The chief items were a Piano and Cello Sonata by Strauss – not so bad – and a gorgeous concerto for two pianos of Bach's. The latter was

[3] Cambridge University Musical Club, organized by undergraduates. Later, see entry for 23 October 1912, there is mention also of CUMS or Cambridge University Musical Society, run by junior and senior members of the university.

splendid and very well performed. I came away at 9.45 with Wittgenstein, and went with him to his rooms, where I stayed till 11.30. He was very communicative and told me lots about himself: that for nine years, till last Xmas, he suffered from terrific loneliness*: that he continually thought of suicide then, and felt ashamed of never daring to kill himself: he put it that he had had 'a hint that he was *de trop* in this world', but that he had meanly disregarded it. He had been brought up to engineering, for which he had neither taste nor talent. And only recently he had tried philosophy and come up here to study under Russell which had proved his salvation: for Russell had given him encouragement. Russell, I know, has a high opinion of him: and has been corrected by him and convinced that he§ was wrong in one or two points of philosophy: and Russell is not the only philosophical don up here that Wittgenstein has convinced of error. Wittgenstein has few hobbies, which rather accounts for his loneliness. One can't thrive entirely on big and important pursuits like Triposes. But he is quite interesting and pleasant: I fancy he has quite got over his morbidness now.

* mental – not physical.
§ = Russell.

Monday, June 3rd, 1912

Then went to chapel and read the lesson. Wittgenstein also came to chapel – specially to hear me!

Tuesday, June 4th, 1912

At 4.45 I went to the Union[4] and later called on Wittgenstein: I have accepted his Iceland scheme. Mother and Father see no objection, and it seems as if it would be rather fun.

[4] The university debating society with clubroom and restaurant.

Thursday, June 6th, 1912

At 1.45 I went *chez* Wittgenstein and afterwards on to the Laboratory for more experiments. Came back at 3.15 to my rooms.

Friday, June 7th, 1912

After the concert I met Wittgenstein and he came up to my rooms till 12.0.

Monday, July 1st, 1912

Later I dined at Buol's, and afterwards called on Wittgenstein: He was working, so I did not stay for long.*

* He has not gone down since last term, but has stayed up all the time.

Tuesday, July 2nd, 1912

At 4.30. I went to tea with Wittgenstein. I came away at 6.0.

Wednesday, July 3rd, 1912

At 4.30 Wittgenstein came to tea. He left at 6.30 about.

Friday, July 12th, 1912

At 4.0. I went to tea with Wittgenstein: later I went out and helped him to interview a lot of furniture at various shops: he is moving into college next term. It was rather amusing: he is terribly fastidious and we led the shopman a frightful dance, Wittgenstein ejaculating 'No – Beastly!' to 90 per cent of what he shewed us!

Saturday, July 13th, 1912

At 6.30 I went *chez* Wittgenstein and we went out and dined together at the Bull Hotel. Afterwards we strolled about and explored some new laboratory buildings in the course of construction. Finally we returned to his rooms. I came away at 9.

Sunday, July 14th, 1912

Hall 7.50. Afterwards Pam[5] and Wittgenstein came *chez moi* – the latter to hear Pam and I make a hideous hash of Schubert's Unfinished Symphony as a duet! Wittgenstein departed at about 9.0.

Monday, July 15th, 1912

At 5.0 Wittgenstein came to tea: later I accompanied him over some shopping. He goes down tonight – back to Austria, so I said 'au Revoir', till we meet again before starting for Iceland.

Thursday, September 5th, 1912

At 4.15 I set out with luggage in a cab for New St[6] and eventually caught the 5.0 train to Euston. It arrived punctually at 7.0, and Wittgenstein met me on the platform. After extracting my luggage we got into a taxi and drove to the

[5] Eric A. Pam of Clare College left Cambridge after one year.
[6] New Street Station, Birmingham.

Grand Hotel, Trafalgar Square. I tried to suggest some less pretentious hotel – especially as Wittgenstein is staying with Russell in any case – but he would not hear of it! There is to be no sparing of expense on this trip! There was a telegram for Wittgenstein when we arrived at the hotel, from his brother, who has just returned from Iceland, saying that the weather there is exceptionally cold, and that he advises the project to be abandoned: which very nearly did persuade Wittgenstein to give up the whole scheme: however I did, by great tact and persuasion, persuade him back again. Then we proceeded to financial arrangements: Wittgenstein, or rather his father, insists on paying for both of us: I had expected him to be pretty liberal – but he surpassed all my expectations: Wittgenstein handed me over £145 in notes, and kept the same amount in notes himself. He also has a letter of Credit for about £200! After these transactions we adjourned to the 'Grill Room' and dined. Then we went out for a stroll – on the embankment mostly. We strolled about till 10.45, ending up at Russell's rooms, where I left Wittgenstein: I returned to the Hotel by tube to Trafalgar Square.

Friday, September 6th, 1912

Got up at 7.30 – had breakfast at 8.0 – and finally left the Hotel in a taxi at 8.30 for King's Cross. There I met Wittgenstein, and we caught the 9.0 am train to Cambridge – where he has some business, connected mostly with the new rooms he is going into next term. I need hardly say we travelled first class! Got to Cambridge at 10.30 and having left our luggage in the cloak room took a taxi into the town. Our sundry and various business occupied us till 12.0, when we took another taxi back to the station. Thence we caught the 12.25 train to Ely – changed there and reached Peterborough at about 2.0. Here we had a beastly trouble about our luggage: it had been labelled 'Peterborough', but there are two stations there – first the G[reat] E[astern] Ry and then further on the G[reat] N[orthern] Ry. We went on to the latter, and then discovered that our luggage had been put out at the former. However we got a cab, drove back and fetched it successfully. We also called at the Post Office for a telegram from the steamship Co. at Leith, saying that our boat starts at 9.0 tomorrow night: we had wired from Cambridge for this information telling them to reply to Telegraph Restant Peterborough.

We had lunch at the GN Hotel at Peterborough, and then caught the 3.10 train on to Grantham. There we changed once more into the Scotch express: it left at 4.25, and eventually reached Edinburgh at 10.45 pm – stopping only at York, Darlington, Newcastle and Berwick. Had tea and dinner on the train. Quite a comfortable journey. From the station at Edinburgh we drove to the Caledonian Hotel, but they had no rooms empty: however we telephoned from there to the Royal Hotel, and they said they had rooms: so we drove back thither. Got to bed finally about 11.30.

Saturday, September 7th, 1912

Wittgenstein and I breakfasted independently – he at 10.0 and I at 9.0. Later I called at the Post Office for letters and got two from Mother. Later Wittgenstein and I went out shopping: he is being very fussy about taking enough clothing: he himself has three bags of luggage, and is much perturbed by my single box. He made me buy a second rug in Cambridge and several other odds and ends in Edinburgh this morning: I have resisted a good deal – especially as it is not my money I am thus spending. I got my own back on him, however, by inducing him to buy oilskins which he had not got.

Later we took trams down to Leith – made sundry arrangements about tickets on the boat – and visited the boat herself – the 'Sterling'. She much resembles an ordinary Cross Channel steamer, and her smallness disgusted Wittgenstein greatly: but he calmed down later. We returned to our hotel for lunch. After wards we did more shopping. Had dinner at the Hotel at 6.0, and at 6.30 left it in a cab for Leith. We had to carry our own luggage on board, as there was no one about! We got settled in pretty soon. We have each a two berthed cabin to ourselves – small, but not bad.

We weighed anchor at 9.0. It poured with rain all the evening, but we walked about on deck till 10.0. There was a sort of light tea at 9.0 – in the saloon. At 10.0 Wittgenstein went to bed. I stayed up another ¾ hour talking to two men – passengers – one of them returning to his home in the Faeroe Islands – and the other going to Iceland as a commercial traveller, I suppose. Both speak English imperfectly. There are about 10 passengers on board – including several ladies: but as far as I know, no English but myself. Of course the boat is Danish and comes from Copenhagen.

Sunday, September 8th, 1912

Got up at 6.0 and found ourselves off the coast of Scotland – the boat pitching slightly. Had breakfast at 7.30 and then spent a long time writing this diary. Wittgenstein got up about 9.0: later we sat up on deck together: the rain had by this time cleared off. Lunch was at 11.0 – consisting of heaps of sausagy sorts of things, cold, laid on the table to be chosen from. Afterwards we strummed on the piano – for there is one on the ship – mostly Schubert songs, of which we have an edition with us. Later we sat on deck and watched some passengers and the Captain play 'deck-quoits': the latter is a pleasant burly individual and speaks English quite well.

Dinner was at 4.30. Afterwards we steered between the Orkney Isles and the mainland, which was interesting. Tea at 7.0 – soon after which I went to bed.

The boat pitched slightly all day, but I did not ever feel

sick. Wittgenstein did not feel very well, but was never actually sick.

Monday, September 9th, 1912

Got up at 7.0: it was much rougher by now, and showery outside. Breakfast 7.30. Wittgenstein stayed in bed all day – feeling very sick – though he was never actually so. I did my best to attend to him, but, towards the end of the day especially, I did not feel too well myself. I played the piano a bit in the morning. During most of the afternoon I lay down in my cabin – and likewise after dinner. The hours of meals were same as yesterday. Finally about 8.30 – just after visiting Wittgenstein – I returned to my cabin and was sick at once. Then I got into bed and immediately went to sleep!

Tuesday, September 10th, 1912

We reached the Faeroe Isles – Thorshavn – at 1.0 am I got up and went on deck, but there was not much to be seen. Got up again at 6.0. It was beautifully fine and sunny, and the Faeroe Isles very beautiful – high and mountainy and of the quaintest and boldest shapes. We weighed anchor again at 7.0. After breakfast at 7.30 – Wittgenstein having got up – we sat up together on deck. It was much calmer today – though the ship still pitched a good deal. I felt nothing whatever of sickness: I think Wittgenstein did toward the end of the day; he went to bed early. During the morning I converted my cabin into a dark room and developed six films I had taken on board: unfortunately I underdeveloped – otherwise they were good.[7] In the afternoon both Wittgenstein and I played deck-quoits with the other passengers.

[7] None of the numerous pictures taken by Pinsent on the journeys to Iceland and Norway has survived.

Later it clouded over and we all went below. At the request of the other passengers I played the piano a bit. Went to bed about 9.0.

Wednesday, September 11th, 1912

During the morning – after 7.30 breakfast – I printed the films I developed yesterday: I did not tone them however. The ship continued to pitch and roll a good deal, but I felt nothing: I seem to have got over it. Wittgenstein is still bad, though curiously he has never yet been actually sick: he got up about 10.0 and we sat on deck together. After lunch all the passengers came on deck and we all – except Wittgenstein, who was too sick,* and eventually about 3.30 retired to bed below – played the most childish of games – 'tick' and so forth – great fun and splendid exercise. The other passengers are all of them Icelandic, but can mostly speak English: they consist of a Reykjavik merchant and his wife – returning from a business voyage§: he is very talkative and asks me the price of everything I possess! There is also the young man I mentioned on Saturday (the one mentioned second; the former of course got off at Faeroe) – and also a Mrs Schmidt – young and pretty – I don't know where her husband is – and two spinsters – one young one middle-aged. They are all very sociable and naïvely amused by childish things and altogether very agreeable. After dinner we played 'Old maid' in the saloon. Went to bed about 10.0.

* i.e. felt sick: he was never actually sick during the whole voyage.

§ Named Müller

Thursday, September 12th, 1912

It was quite rough during the night and up to 10 am – after which we got under shelter in Reykjavik bay. I did not

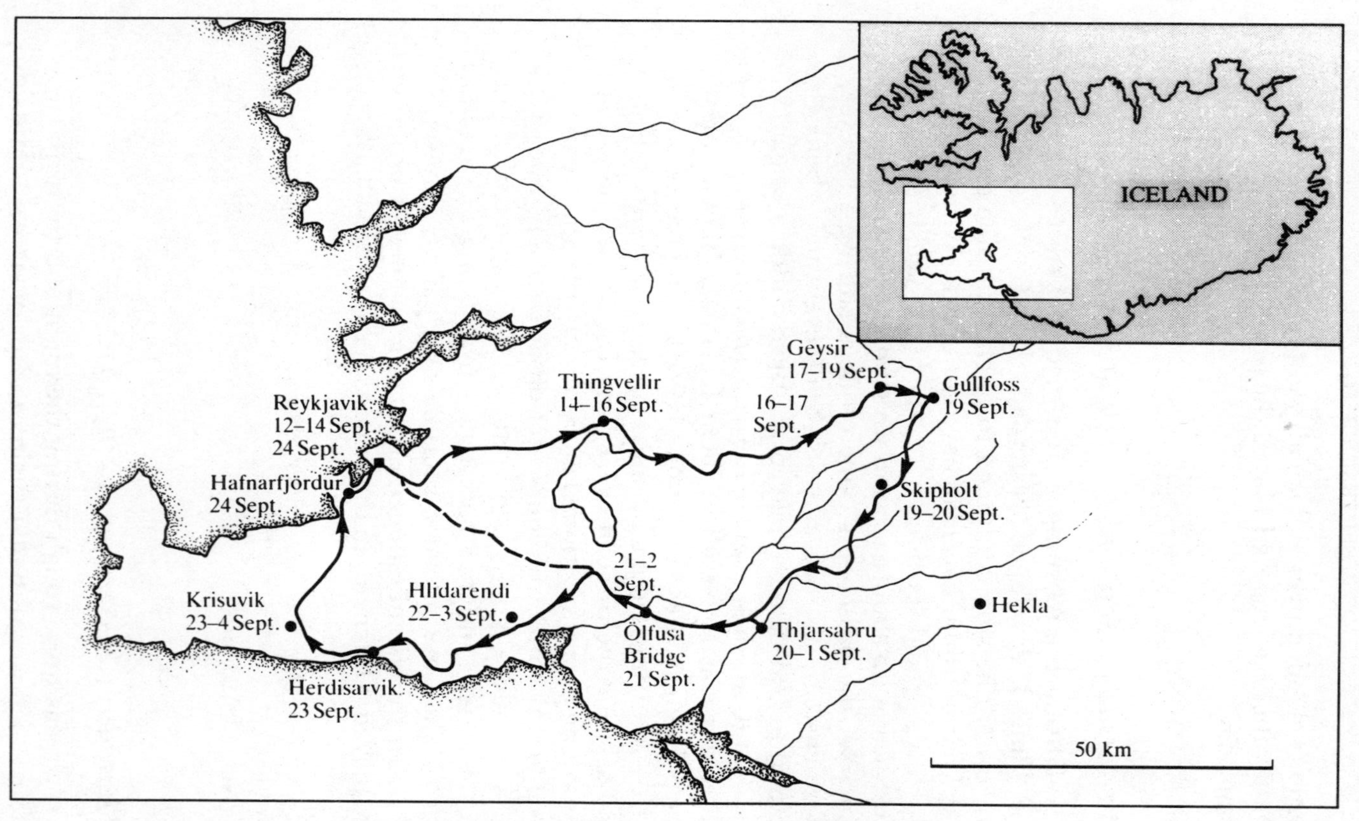

Wittgenstein's and Pinsent's itinerary in Iceland.

feel a bit ill: got up at 7.30 and after breakfast packed up my things. Wittgenstein got up about 10.0: it was drizzling and foggy outside. Lunch at 11.0 as usual. We anchored in Reykjavik about 1.0, and after a terrific hurry and fuss were put ashore in a small boat – our luggage likewise – and repaired to the 'Hotel Reykjavik'. We had lunch soon after at 2.30 about. The Hotel was big and quite comfortable – much like what Guide books would call a 'second class' hotel in England or the Continent. After lunch we arranged with a guide – introduced by the Hotel Proprietor – about journeying inland: (we had no trouble about finding a guide – in fact we were touted as soon as we got on shore!). His name was Jónson and he seemed quite a pleasant fellow and talked English quite well, so we took him on and arranged several details with him. Later we went out for a walk in Reykjavik. Reykjavik is really a wonderful place: it is fairly big – population 11,600 – and has broad streets, shops where one can buy almost anything, and many of the most up-to-date comforts of civilization: for instance there is a gas-works and almost every house has its telephone. I saw several men going about on bicycles. The houses are all built of corrugated iron on stone foundations, and are somewhat gaudily painted – mostly red or yellow: the general effect is quaint and not a bit unpleasing. The prices of things in the shops are ridiculously low – in some cases about a quarter of what would be paid in England. The natives are a robust, healthy looking lot, as a rule very educated: almost all of them speak English quite well, and probably German and French also – as well as Danish and Icelandic – the languages of the country. They look prosperous – and slums and the squalor of English towns are quite absent.

The weather was dull and slightly cold – though not nearly so cold as I expected. Wittgenstein and I had an animated discussion on public schools – eventually getting quite angry with each other until we found that we had both misunderstood the other. He has an enormous horror of what he calls a 'Philistine' attitude towards cruelty and suffering – any callous attitude – and accuses Kipling of such: and he got the idea that I sympathised with it.

We had supper at 7.30. Afterwards I smoked and wrote letters. Bed 10.30.

Friday, September 13th, 1912

Got up at 8.0 and went out and took a photo. in the town. Then came in and wrote this diary till breakfast at 9.0. Then went out with Wittgenstein and did some shopping and took several photos. in the town. We came back to the Hotel at 11.0 and met our Guide, and he took us round buying sundry necessaries for journeying inland – tinned food *etc.* Later we went to a bank and deposited the greater part of the money we had with us – until we should get back from our tour. We also went to the office of a steamship co. to secure berths home: the man there understood us imperfectly and was a bit of a fool, but I think we persuaded him what we meant: Wittgenstein however got terribly fussy and talked about our not getting home at all, and I got quite irritated with him: eventually he went off alone and got a man from the bank to act as interpreter and go through the whole business again at the steamship office.

We had lunch at 2.15. Afterwards I went to a photographic shop and hired a dark-room and developed six films there – quite successful. Wittgenstein came with me. Then we posted several letters: I am afraid, however, that they won't go till Sept. 18th. Then we went for a stroll, finally returning to the photo. shop to fetch the films, which had been washing. We returned to the hotel then and packed travelling necessities in boxes specially fitted to the pack-saddles of the pack-ponies we shall use: we packed up all we shall not require to be stored at the Hotel during our absence. Supper was at 7.15. The guide called at 8.0 – about some detail. Bed 10.30.

Saturday, September 14th, 1912

Got up at 8.0 and finished off packing. Breakfast at 9.0. The guide was to be round with ponies at 10.0 – but he was half an hour late: there was a lot more delay before we finally left Reykjavik – shoeing ponies *etc* – in fact Icelanders are a very dilatory people – but we got off finally about 12.0. Our cortège consisted of Wittgenstein, the guide and myself each on a pony: and in front we drove the two pack ponies and three spare ponies:* the guide displayed immense skill in heading off any pony which left the road and generally in keeping them all together. The ponies are small and shaggy – with a short trot: we rode at the trot on and on almost the whole time – rather tiring. It was a misty drizzly day and we wore our oilskins – trousers and all – and looked very Arctic! After about 12 Kilom. we got off for 15 mins. to rest the ponies: about 3 Kilom. further on we had lunch at an inn – eggs and bread and butter. At about 35 Kilom. we changed our mounts for the spares. Our destination – Thingvellir – is 50 Kilom. and we reached it about 7.0 and went to the Inn there. We appear to have done the distance in exceptionally fast time. The country through which we passed is excessively bleak – moorlands covered with lava-stones and what in England would be heather. The latter is of the most glorious colours – light green, yellow and pink – and even in the misty weather we had looked almost vivid. The road was not hilly, though there were mountains in the distance. Towards the end we descended upon the Thingvellir lake – which is surrounded by volcanic-looking hills and looked magnificent. Thingvellir can hardly be called a village, as it consists entirely of a church, a parsonage, the inn and a few scattered farms. The inn was quite comfortable and we soon got a good supper of trout and bread and butter and marmalade. Afterwards I had a most interesting evening with Wittgenstein: he taught me Russell's definition of Number *etc* and the use of his logical symbolism – excessively interesting. Wittgenstein makes a very good teacher. We went to bed about 10.30.

Our guide I always thought pleasant, but he improves upon acquaintance. He is quite intelligent and does lots of odd jobs for us willingly and without being asked.[§] And he can talk – in English – quite interestingly.

* Quite loosed and in no way fastened either to us or to each other.

§ He is very useful as an interpreter.

Sunday, September 15th, 1912

We decided to spend today here at Thingvellir. Had breakfast at 9.30 and later explored the surrounding neighbourhood on foot. It was rainy during the morning, but it cleared up a bit – though still showery in the afternoon. The country here is all heather on rocks – and is intersected by great gullies – with perpendicular rocky sides and gorgeous purple-blue water at the bottom. Some of these gullies are as much as 50 ft deep in places,* and what makes them all the more extraordinary is that except for them the surrounding land is quite flat. After a preliminary exploration I came back to the Inn and fetched my Camera and then went out again and took 3 Photos. We came in for lunch at 1.30. I went out for a short time in the afternoon with Wittgenstein, but soon left him to his own devices and returned to the inn and wrote this Diary. We had a huge supper at 5.0 (Lunch had consisted only of bread and butter and marmalade – with cocoa).

We had some quite exciting rock climbing to do this morning in the course of our explorations: I am not very good myself – but Wittgenstein is terribly nervous. His fussiness comes out here again – he is always begging me not to risk my life! It is funny that he should be like that – for otherwise he is quite a good travelling companion.

In the course of the afternoon there arrived 4 men – from Geysir – whom we found afterwards to be Swiss: we got these to take some letters for us and post them in Reykjavik – whither they were going tomorrow.

One thing I forgot to mention about our Icelandic ponies is their extraordinary sure-footedness: they thread their way over the roughest boulder-stricken ground – at the trot – in the most wonderful manner: and on roads covered with loose stones they do exactly what they like!

* and about 10 yds wide.

Monday, September 16th, 1912

Got up at 7.30 and packed. Had a huge breakfast – three courses – at 8.30. We got off finally, on our ponies, at about 9.45. The weather cleared up quite fine and sunny, though it became distinctly colder, especially on high ground. We crossed the Thingvellir plain – along the top end of the lake – and then gradually climbed up for about an hour – going very slowly partly owing to hilliness and partly to the rough and wet state of the ground. The road from Reykjavik was quite a carriage-road, but today it became no more than a track. At the top of our climb we inspected a curious big boulder with a deep crater in it, extending quite deep down into the earth. Next we descended down into a big plain, with very picturesque mountains on the left. There I got off and changed spools in my camera: I had already taken two photo., and then and later I took two more. We crossed the plain – going faster now – and finally, about 2.30 pm, reached a farm, where we had lunch. The food was rough but quite edible: the only thing I did not much care for was their 'black' bread – very heavy and a bit tough. We set off again at 3.45 about and rode – with only one halt, fairly fast – till 7.30, when we got to a farm about an hour's ride short of Geysir. We had intended to get to Geysir tonight, but as it was getting dark we decided to put up here instead. We should have got on much quicker, I fancy, if it had not been for the wet state of the ground. The quarters we got at the farm were quite comfortable: we managed to get beds in separate rooms, though Wittgenstein's was somewhat of a makeshift; however he says it was quite comfortable. We were very sleepy when we got in, and after a big meal served at 9.0, both retired to rest.

It was very clear today and on the way one saw the snow mountains – including Hekla – quite distinctly. This evening, about 8.30, we saw the Aurora Borealis – looking like streaks of dull white light in the sky towards the North.

Tuesday, September 17th, 1912

Got up at 8.0 – quite refreshed and hardly a bit stiff after yesterday's great exertions. Breakfast did not appear till 10.0 – as I have said the Icelanders are a very dilatory lot! We started on our ponies about 10.30 and rode on, very slowly, to Geysir, where we arrived about 12.0. It was fine and sunny again this morning, though it got misty and drizzly by the evening. We went to the Inn at Geysir and put up there: then went out and examined the hot springs. The place is full of little wells with bubbling boiling water steaming out – smelling strongly of H_2S! Most of them merely bubble continuously, but two of them send up periodic great fountains: of the latter the littler one does so once or twice a day, and I photographed it, when about 2.30 pm it did so. We encouraged it to spout by stopping up the hole with turf – apparently a recognized method. The spout it sent up rose about 15 feet high amid clouds of steam. The bigger Geysir only spouts once every few days, and as it has not done so for 5 days now, we hope it will soon: apparently it rises some 130 feet and must look very fine.

We had lunch at 1.30, and afterwards – as I mentioned above watched the little Geysir spouting. The rest of the day we waited for the big Geysir to spout: there were, once or twice, subterranean gurgles heard, which always occur before it spouts, but nothing happened. Wittgenstein and I went for a stroll together up a little hill close by. Supper was served at 5.30. Later we went for another stroll. Later he taught me a lot more of Russell's symbolic Logic. In the middle of that the big Geysir suddenly began gurgling again and we rushed out in the mist and dark, but nothing happened! Went to bed about 9.30 pm.

Wednesday, September 18th, 1912

Got up at 8.0 and had breakfast at 8.30. After breakfast Wittgenstein was suddenly seized with violent stomach ache: but luckily it went off after about an hour. He may have got a small chill, and anyhow the big Geysir has not yet spouted, so we are staying here today. Later in the morning I wrote this diary. We had lunch about 1.30. Afterwards I went for a walk by myself, but not for long. The weather was dull and misty. I also read a good deal of Wuthering Heights, which I have been reading on and off during this journey. About 4.0. Wittgenstein and I went for a walk together – and talked Logic most of the while. We had supper about 6.0. Later we talked a great deal of Symbolic Logic: I am learning a lot from him. He is really remarkably clever: I have never yet been able to find the smallest fault in his reasoning: and he has made me reconstruct entirely my ideas on several subjects.

Thursday, September 19th, 1912

Breakfast at 9.0. At 10.15 we set out. We have not seen the big Geysir erupt – but we can't wait any longer! Wittgenstein gave the lady of the Inn a somewhat substantial tip when we left, and she came up to each of us and shook hands – most quaint! They are always shaking hands here – our guide does so with almost every one he meets!

It cleared up this morning, though the ground was still very wet and we had to go very slowly as far as the Gullfoss waterfall – where we arrived at 12.30.* We spent half an hour there. It is really quite a big one and very fine. After leaving Gullfoss we progressed quicker and at 1.30 halted at a farm for lunch: they could only provide coffee and black bread, but we added tinned meat and plates and knives and forks of our own and made quite a pleasant picnic in the open air. We set out again at 3.0. The country we passed through today was much less bleak and more green than hitherto. At 5.15 – after a quick ride – we reached the farm of Skipholt, where we put up for the night. We got extremely comfortable quarters indeed – the farm is the biggest I have seen yet in Iceland. We had supper at 6.45, and later talked philosophy *etc* till 10.0 – when I went to bed.

The Aurora Borealis was visible again tonight quite plainly.

Wittgenstein has been talking a lot, at different times, about 'Philistines' – a name he gives to all people he dislikes.[§] I think some of the views I have expressed have struck him as a bit philistine**, and he is rather puzzled because he does not consider me really a Philistine – and I don't think he dislikes me! He satisfies himself by saying that I shall think differently as soon as I am a bit older!

The farm we are in tonight is typical of all I have seen in Iceland. They seem to lay themselves out to a certain extent to receive travellers like us: there is usually a separate entrance for us, and one or two rooms which are never used by anyone except such as we. Charges are low – usually about 6/- for supper, bed and breakfast, each. Otherwise the farmers support themselves mostly, as far as I see, on sheep rearing. They grow no corn – merely hay and a few vegetables.

* The roads today were mere bridle-paths – much as on Monday last.

§ Vide supra – Thursday Sept. 12th.

** Views – that is – on practical things – not on philosophy – for instance on the advantage of this age over past ages and so forth.

Friday, September 20th, 1912

Up at 8.0. Breakfast 9.30. We got off at 11.0 and rode fairly fast till 2.0, when we reached a big farm down in a plain, where we had lunch. This farmer seemed to be a very cultured man – he had quite a lot of books. It had been fine when we started, but about 3.30 it started raining: by the evening there was a regular gale and quite a downpour. We rode from 3.0 to 7.0 over the dullest of marshy plains – along a straight road* – through this rain, and eventually reached Thjorsabru Inn very damp. We got rooms and changed and had supper about 8.30. Went to bed about 10.0.

* Before lunch the roads were simply paths – afterwards however they were quite like 'carriage roads'.

Saturday, September 21st, 1912

Got up at 8.0. Breakfast at 9.30. We started about 11.15. The sky was still quite overcast, but it did not rain – though it blew hard – during the morning. We rode along the road – quite a good carriage road – till 2.0, when we reached the Ölfusa Bridge, and there we entered the inn for lunch. They took a whole hour getting it ready, but it was good when it came – trout it consisted of. We got off again about 4.0 and rode on very fast for an hour to an Inn just 50 Kilom. from Reykjavik, where we put up for the night.* After about half an hour's delay they shewed us our rooms: and after changing I wrote this diary. Supper was at 7.30. Afterwards till 10.0 I read Wuthering Heights. Wittgenstein was a bit sulky all the evening: he is very sensitive if I get, momentarily, a bit irritated over some trifle – as I did tonight – I forget what about: the result being that he was depressed and silent for the rest of the evening. He is always imploring me not to be irritable: and I do my best, and really, I think, I have not been so often this trip!

* It began to rain, and blow harder than ever about 3.0, and we rode this hour right through the storm.

Sunday, September 22nd, 1912

It rained and blew terribly all night. We had breakfast at 9.30. Then decided that, in any case, we would go no further than Hlitharendi today, and that, as that is only 4 hrs. ride, we would wait till after lunch, to give the weather a chance of clearing. We spent the morning indoors reading and playing chess. Had an early lunch at 12.45. Our hopes with regard to the weather were realised: we set out at 1.15, and it started to clear at that very moment: the sky became eventually quite blue – though hazy. The route left the high road to Reykjavik after about a mile and then became very rough and stony for a while, and we had to go very slowly: later it got better – though still a mere path – and we got on quicker. We reached the farm Hlitharendi about 5.15 pm. Had supper at 7.0. Our quarters here are the poorest we have had: usually we get two bedrooms and the parlour as private sitting and dining room: here Wittgenstein's bed was in the parlour itself and my bedroom exceedingly small, and dark. However it was quite comfortable.

After supper Wittgenstein taught me more symbolic Logic. Quite interesting: and he teaches very well.

Monday, September 23rd, 1912

Got up 7.15 and had breakfast at 8.30. We got off at 9.0. It was fairly fine at first: the way was rough to an extreme the whole of today: quite 9/10 ths of it we had to walk* over lava plains, where there was no path whatever – simply: periodic heaps of stones to indicate the way. The ground covered with huge and small boulders of lava – dark black cindery stone – and the ponies literally climbing over them: or else a desert of volcanic lava dust – black sand – into which the ponies' feet sunk inches, making very heavy work for them. We reached the farm Herdisarvik about 1.30 and had lunch there: supplying tinned corned beef out of our own store. About 10.30 it suddenly began pelting with rain, and for about half an hour pelted without intermission: then it cleared up altogether. Our oilskins however kept us quite dry: indeed they are wonderfully efficient; I have only once had to change clothes through wet: and then because I refused to put the trousers on till it was too late to be worth while!

We set out again after lunch about 2.45 and reached Krisuvik at 5.45 pm. Just at the end we got a mile of sharp trotting, which was gloriously exhilarating after hours of walking. Put up at the farm for the night: very comfortable quarters. At 6.0 Wittgenstein and I went for a walk up a curious isolated hill close by, whence one got quite a fine view. We had a long discussion about plans for tomorrow: I wanted to go straight back to Reykjavik and he to stay a day here and go on on Wednesday: at first I gave in to him and said we would stay here two nights: but he got very worried about my concession (eventually we hit upon the compromise we actually carried out): he is morbidly afraid of my giving in just 'to get a little peace' and so forth: of course that was not my motive: I did so as a favour to him and in order not to be selfish: I think I persuaded him so in the end. We came in for supper about 7.30. Afterwards talked about lots of things – not philosophy this time!

* *i.e.* we rode the ponies but they walked.

Tuesday, September 24th, 1912

I got the guide to call me at 6.45, and got up and went to the top of that hill again to take some photos: Came back for breakfast at 8.30. We set off at 9.15 and reached the hot springs *etc*, that Wittgenstein wanted to see here*, about 10.0. Spent two hours examining them: mostly sulphur – with quite a lot of pure sulphur lying quite close to the surface. We set out again for Reykjavik at 12.0. The weather was gloriously fine. The ride was one of the most interesting we have had: the road as far as Hafnarfjördur a path and afterwards a good carriage road. We first ascended very steeply, then crossed two extinct volcanic craters, and then descended again into the plain. At 1.15 we had lunch off corned beef and chocolate – picnicking. There was not a single farm until Hafnarfjördur. We set out again at 1.45 and reached Hafnarfjördur at 5.0 – after travelling very fast all the time except a few places where the ground was very rough. Hafnarfjördur is a fishing village and we had cocoa and bread at a sort of café there: we set out again at 5.30 and rode fairly fast into Reykjavik by 7.0. We went back to the Hotel Reykjavik. Supper was at 8.0. We were alone last time we stayed here, but now there are four other visitors. To one – a very splendid bounder – I talked during supper, and afterwards Wittgenstein and I had a long discussion about such people: he simply won't speak to them, but really, I think, they are rather amusing. Later I had a bath: did not get to bed till almost 1.0 am. A very long day, but I was not a bit tired. It was pleasant to sleep once more in a bed of reasonable length: the beds in farms *etc* were one and all too short: moreover they make them with sheets and a 'duvet' only – a horrid method: luckily we both had two rugs with us and could therefore dispense with the 'duvet'.

The two following observations come in here as well as elsewhere: firstly I don't believe there is a single tree in Iceland: I have not seen one. Secondly, I have said Icelanders are dilatory: they are also noisy. They talk always very loud, and when they shut a door they slam it – invariably! Otherwise they are extremely nice people.

Our inland journey has been very successful, and I think Wittgenstein thinks so too. I am quite sorry it is over.

* It was for these he wished to stay here two nights.

Wednesday, September 25th, 1912

Had breakfast at 9.0. Afterwards I did a little shopping: also wrote this diary. At 11.0 the guide came to fetch away our boxes (the ones we used travelling) and to be paid: we gave him about £2 tip: I think he deserved it as he was certainly very efficient and a thoroughly nice companionable man. Later I went on writing this diary. I also fetched a letter from the post office – one from Mother and written from Plymouth on their way home from Falmouth[8] in the car: dated Sept. 7th. I hope to get more letters on Friday – when the next boat from England arrives.

Later Wittgenstein made an awful fuss: he has taken so violent a dislike to the bounder, mentioned yesterday, (though he has never spoken to him) that he refuses to eat at the same table with him! So we gave orders that our meals should be served an hour before table d'hôte in all cases – a thing not so absurd as might be thought, as table d'hôte hours are all ridiculously late – breakfast 10.0, lunch 3.0, and supper 8.0. That succeeded all right at breakfast this morning, but they forgot all about it at lunch. Wittgenstein and I went out to see if we could get anything in Reykjavik, but failed: eventually he ate a few biscuits up in his room: I went to the table d'hôte!

At 4.0 I went to the same photo. shop I patronized before and developed 30 films I had taken travelling inland. Fairly satisfactory except for one roll of six – all of which I under-developed through forgetting to renew the developer. I tried my best – went on developing for hours, but it was no use. I think 75 per cent of the whole 30 should make good prints. Got back to the hotel by 6.30 – having left the films to be washed and dried – and found Wittgenstein still fairly sulky about the lunch business. However we got our supper all right at 7.0, and had champagne (very sweet!) which cheered him up a bit, finally leaving him quite normal: later we went for a stroll round the town.

Thursday, September 26th, 1912

After breakfast we walked up to the Photo. shop, whence I fetched my films. Then returned to the Hotel and

[8] The Pinsents had been on holiday in Cornwall.

spent an hour filing them into my negative book. At 11.0 we went out and made arrangements about cabins on the 'Botnia' tomorrow. The guide appeared at 12.0 and took us over the Reykjavik National Museum, quite interesting – with lots of pre-historic relics. Came in to lunch at 2.30 pm.

Earlier in the morning we met Mr Müller (whose acquaintance we made on the 'Sterling') in a street, and he asked us to coffee *chez lui* tonight at 9.0: very pleasant of him.

After lunch I talked with Wittgenstein and a new visitor to the hotel – an Englishman who, with a friend, also at the hotel has sailed over hither in a ketch: he is going back however by the steamer tomorrow – having sent his ketch home separately. Quite a pleasant man, as also is his friend, whom I also met in the course of the day.

Later we did some shopping. We had supper at 7.0. Today is the birthday of the King of Denmark, and consequently there was a big public dinner tonight at the hotel – beautiful foreign consuls mostly in magnificent uniforms. They got very merry before the night was over. At 9.0 pm Wittgenstein and I went *chez* Mr Müller: Mr Müller was there also. We stayed till 10.45 and had quite a pleasant evening. Mr Müller is quite amusing.

Friday, September 27th, 1912

After breakfast I went to the Post Office and fetched two letters for myself from Mother – the second dated September 19th – mostly about Sid's[9] wedding and the journey home from Falmouth. Then walked with Wittgenstein towards the Reykjavik hot springs: but eventually we decided to be independent, and he went on to the springs, and I sat on a wall and read my letters and then returned to the hotel by myself. He came in for lunch at 2.30 pm. Later I went out for a stroll by myself. At 4.45 the guide appeared, having

[9] Sidney Pinsent (1878–1967), engineer, later in business in Argentina, David Pinsent's first cousin.

arranged everything for getting us and our luggage aboard the 'Botnia': we put off from the quay in a small boat, boarded the 'Botnia' and took possession of our cabins: there was some fuss at first about my having my trunk in my cabin: but luckily the guide knew the Captain of the 'Botnia' and arranged it satisfactorily! The guide went ashore about 6.0, having said 'Good-bye' to us. We were due to start at 6.0, but did not get off till 7.0. eventually. At 8.0 there was dinner in the saloon: soon afterwards I went to bed.

The 'Botnia' is a larger boat than the 'Sterling' and more comfortable: there are about 30 first class passengers, half of them English.* The six others besides ourselves, who stayed at the Hotel Reykjavik, are there. As before Wittgenstein and I have got a 2-berth cabin each to ourselves.

* The other half include the Prime Minister of Iceland.

Saturday, September 28th, 1912

The sea was not very rough and I slept well and was not sick. At 7.0 am. we reached the islands Vestmannaeyjar – where we called. I got up at 7.30 and had breakfast. Wittgenstein, also having not felt sick, got up at 8.0. We remained at Vestmannaeyjar till 11.0 – during most of which time I printed photographs. Lunch at 11.0 in the saloon. Later I lay down in my bunk and read 'Wuthering Heights' for an hour, eventually finishing it: a good book, though I think a bit melodramatic: Heathcliff is absurd, though better earlier in the story than at the end – more natural and comprehensible, that is.

Later I printed more photos. and then toned all I had done – eighteen of them: a difficult business as the ship was rolling all the time! Dinner was served at 5.30 pm. Sat next to and talked with an English gentleman, not hitherto mentioned, a middle aged genial man – with a lot of sceptical common sense. Later I paced the deck for half an hour with another Englishman, not yet mentioned – a young medical student: apparently he and his friend followed us round Thingvellir, Geysir *etc* – a day behind all the while. They took no luggage and only one spare pony and were very contemptuous of our huge cavalcade!

Later I visited Wittgenstein for an hour before going to bed: he was sick this afternoon and has kept his cabin since.

Sunday, September 29th, 1912

Got up at 7.30 and had breakfast. Wittgenstein got up but lay down mostly all the morning. Did odds and ends till lunch at 11.0. At 1.0 we entered Seydisfjördur, eventually coming alongside the quay at 2.15. A most lovely place – the bay surrounded by huge precipitous mountains. Wittgenstein and I went ashore and strolled about, and I took several photos. Came back on board about 5.0. Dinner at 5.30. Later I converted my cabin into a dark room and developed six films: very fairly good. There was a sort of tea served at 9.0. Later at 10.0 Wittgenstein and I went ashore again and strolled about: the Aurora Borealis was quite visible. We talked Logic mostly, and chiefly about some new research Wittgenstein is doing: I really believe he has discovered something good. Came on board again about 11.0 and went to bed. Some time in the early morning we must have put to sea again – but I was asleep.

Monday, September 30th, 1912

Got up at 7.0 and found the ship entering Reydarfjördur. After breakfast I wrote this diary. Then – the ship having by now got alongside the quay – I went ashore for a stroll with Wittgenstein. We came back about 10.30. Lunch was at 11.0 as usual. We put to sea again at about 12.0, but only went as far as another village in the same fjord, off which we anchored. Waited there till 3.45 loading cargo from boats which put off to us from the shore: they took a long time about it – more so as the men were the slackest and laziest I ever saw! I spent most of the time printing photographs. Tea was served at 3.0. When we finally up-ed anchor at 3.45, we set out straight for Faeroe: it was quite rough outside – the ship rolling a lot. But I never felt the least sick: and nor, I believe, did Wittgenstein. Supper was at 5.30, and a sort of tea, as usual, at 9.0.

Tuesday, October 1st, 1912

Got up at 8.0 and found it rougher than ever. Had breakfast at 8.15. Wittgenstein did not feel sick, but thought it wiser to stay in bed: he got up in the evening when we got to Faeroe. During the morning I finished printing my films. Lunch was at 11.0. Later at about 3.0 we sighted the Faeroe Isles – very impressive, one huge cape falling precipitously about 2,000 ft into the sea, showing dimly and huge about 15 miles away. Later I tried toning some prints: but the ship rolled so much and spilt half the solution, that I had to give it up. The other half of the solution I left in the cabin, and the stewardess poured it away! Supper at 5.30. Soon after we got into calm water – inside the Faeroes – and I tried toning once more, and successfully this time. We anchored off Thorshaven at 6.0 (7.0 English time, which will be used henceforward). Later Wittgenstein got up and we had a long talk in my cabin – mostly on people we knew. 'Tea' at 9.0. Later Wittgenstein and I paced the deck a bit. Later we got round the engineer and visited the engines: Wittgenstein (who has spent a lot of time studying engineering – at Manchester University mostly) explained them to me: very interesting. We witnessed the starting of the ship – in the engine room – when at 11.15 we left Faeroe. Went to bed soon afterwards.

Wednesday, October 2nd, 1912

As soon as we left Faeroe the ship began rolling worse than it has ever done before: my box slid about the cabin, and things had to be very firmly secured. This morning it was no better: but I never felt the least sick: nor did Wittgenstein: he got up. Meals were at the usual hours: most of the rest of the day I spent reading 'No Name' (Wilkie Collins) – trash of the very best kind. We tried pacing the deck at times, but it was too unsteady and cold to be pleasant. At about 6.0 the Orkneys (lighthouse) was sighted. We sailed between them and the Shetlands. That means we have come very quickly from Faeroe – owing to the strong wind behind us.

Thursday, October 3rd, 1912

Got up at 7.0 and packed. We were off Aberdeen now and the sea quite calm again. I had breakfast at 8.30. Lunch 11.0, tea 3.0, as usual. We entered the Firth of Forth about 2.0. One or two naval aeroplanes were sailing about and caused a great sensation on board the 'Botnia'. We got into dock at 5.0 eventually. There was very little bother with customs officials, and we got a cab and drove to the Caledonian Hotel: calling en-route at the Post Office, whence I telegraphed home. At the hotel we had both a huge bath: mine being over first, I employed time booking for our journey on tonight by the 10.50 train – and other details. We dined at 7.45 about – in style with Champagne. Later we went for a stroll together along Prince's Street. Back to the Hotel at 10.0, and on board our train by 10.15. We had sleeping berths and went to bed at once. The train started at 10.50 and went *via* Carlisle and L[ondon] N[orth] W[estern] Ry. We had to change at Crewe at 4.0 am – and the attendant called us at 3.40 according to instructions we had given him. I slept quite well, and was quite surprised when we got to Crewe. Our train on to B'ham was due to leave at 4.30, but was late: moreover it waited still more delay at Stafford: eventually it reached New St at 7.0 – about an hour late.

Friday, October 4th, 1912

We got a cab and drove up to Lordswood.[10] I have persuaded Wittgenstein to stay tonight here – especially as the last concert of the Musical Festival is today, and includes Beethoven's 7th Symphony and Brahms' Requiem. We found a huge party staying at Lordswood. Uncle Bob – just off however – Aunt Bee and Mrs Darwin and of course Porky.[11] Mrs Darwin had suddenly to leave in the course of the morning, owing to bad news about Sir George Darwin.[12] We had breakfast immediately upon our arrival. Afterwards – till 10.45 – I exhibited photographs and generally held forth on the subject of Iceland! At 10.45 Porky and Wittgenstein and I set out by bus for the Town Hall*: we got out into a cab, however, at the Five Ways owing to a panic about getting there in time. The concert began at 10.30: the first part consisted entirely of Brahms' Requiem – simply marvellous and splendidly performed: those climaxes in it are quite indescribable. Wittgenstein said he had never enjoyed it more – and he has heard it pretty often. The chorus was local – the Birmingham Festival Chorus: Henry Wood conducted. Next there was an hour's interval for lunch: we all adjourned to the office (Father's office), where there was a stand up affair: the whole family were there – including Aunt Edith, who is staying at

[10] Name of the Pinsents' house in Birmingham.

[11] The individuals referred to are: Robert John Parker (1857–1918), High Court Judge, cr. Baron Parker of Waddington in 1913, older brother of Ellen Pinsent; Beatrice Craycroft, Ellen's older sister; Ida Darwin, *née* Farrer, wife of the civil engineer Sir Horace Darwin (1851–1928); and Marion Radford ('Porky'), first cousin of David Pinsent.

[12] Sir George Howard Darwin (1845–1912), professor of astronomy and experimental philosophy at Cambridge, second son of Charles Darwin, the naturalist, brother of Horace. He died at Cambridge on 7 December 1912.

Selly Wick.[13] The second half of the Concert began with two selections from Strauss' 'Salome': Wittgenstein refused to go in for them, and stayed outside till the Beethoven, which followed. He went out after that and went back to Lordswood by himself. The 'Salome' was rot, but very clever and amusing in consequence. The Beethoven following was the 7th Symphony – gorgeous. Afterwards a motet of Bach's, 'Be not afraid' – which ended the concert, about 3.30. Father returned to the office and Porky stayed behind to see off Aunt Edith – who is returning to London: so I came back in the motor with Aunt Bee and Mother. Had tea as soon as we got home. Afterwards went with Aunt Bee, Mother, Hester and Wittgenstein for a walk: Wittgenstein had been a bit shy at first, but was easier now and later in the evening altogether at his ease. Dinner at 7.15. Afterwards I got Wittgenstein to explain to Father a lot of the Logic he has been teaching me: I think Father was interested, and certainly he agreed with me afterwards that Wittgenstein is really very clever and acute. Went to bed about 11.0 pm and slept very soundly!

* The rest – except father, who had gone earlier to the office, but joined us at the concert – went in the motor.

Saturday, October 5th, 1912

After breakfast Aunt Bee departed back to London. Later Wittgenstein and Mother and I had a talk on the education of young children – quite interesting. Later Wittgenstein and I played the piano *etc*: we also played the Player-piano: he got quite expert at it by the time he finished. While he played I wrote this diary. Lunch* at 1.30.

[13] Edith Radford, *née* Pinsent, wife of the artist John Radford and David Pinsent's aunt. Selly Wick was the home of David's uncle, Richard Pinsent (later Sir Richard), founder of the firm Pinsent & Co., in whose offices the gathering described took place.

At 2.0 Wittgenstein and I went down to New St station in the motor – (with Peplow,[14] but I drove). I saw him off by the 2.45 train to London.

Thus ends the most glorious holiday I have ever spent! The novelty of the country – of being free of all considerations about economizing – the excitement and everything – all combine to make it the most wonderful experience I have ever had. It leaves almost a mystic-romantic impression on me: for the greatest romance consists in novel sensations – novel surroundings – and so forth, whatever they be provided they are novel. I can only compare my feelings to those I experienced after my 3 months in Lausanne.[15]

* Father got home for lunch.

Saturday, October 12th, 1912

Very little later Wittgenstein appeared: he stayed a long time in my rooms and then I went with him and helped him carry up some furniture – just arrived from London – into his new rooms in Whewell's Court.[16] Later we dined together at Buol's, and afterwards went to an informal concert at the CUMC: it was not very interesting, however, so we came away at 9.0: went for a stroll before returning to Trinity. Soon after I returned to my rooms.

Monday, October 14th, 1912

I went and called on Wittgenstein. Found him slightly more settled in than on Saturday – but still with a lot of his furniture yet to come. He has had his furniture all specially

[14] The Pinsents' gardener-cum-chauffeur.

[15] Pinsent had been there to learn French after leaving Marlborough and before going up to Cambridge.

[16] In Trinity College.

made for him on his own lines – rather quaint but not bad. About 10.30 we set out together, and strolled about the courts of Trinity: eventually we met Russell and he invited us into his rooms. Stayed till 12.15 pm.

Saturday, October 19th, 1912

I met Wittgenstein there[17] and came up to his rooms with him afterwards. Stayed *chez lui* till 11.30 pm.

Wednesday, October 23rd, 1912

At about 3.45 Wittgenstein appeared: he was rather ill with Rheumatism apparently and very sorry for himself. He stayed till 4.30, . . . Hall 7.45 pm. Then to the Guildhall – for a CUMS concert, the programme being Beethoven's Septet and Schubert's Octet. The performance was a bit wooden, but I enjoyed it enormously, especially the Octet. The latter is so wonderfully mystic and romantic. It ended about 10.30 and Wittgenstein, whom I met there, returned with me to my rooms. He stayed till about 11.30 pm. Went to bed when he left.

Thursday, October 24th, 1912

At 10.0 pm. I went *chez* Russell. Wittgenstein was there and also Ritchie[18] and a few others. Somewhat dull at first, though more interesting later on when the conversation got more philosophical. I came away at 12.15.

[17] At a CUMC concert.

[18] A. D. Ritchie (1891–1967), physiologist and philosopher, then Fellow of Trinity College, Cambridge, later Professor of Logic and Metaphysics, University of Edinburgh.

Friday, October 25th, 1912

Wittgenstein called. He explained to me a new solution he has discovered to a problem* which was puzzling him greatly in Iceland, and to which he made a somewhat make-shift solution then. His latest is quite different and covers more ground, and if sound should revolutionize lots of Symbolic Logic: Russell, he says, thinks it is sound, but says nobody will understand it: I think I comprehended it myself however (!). If Wittgenstein's solution works, he will be the first to solve a problem which has puzzled Russell and Frege for some years: it is the most masterly and convincing solution too.

* in the most fundamental Symbolic Logic.

Monday, October 28th, 1912

Worked from 10–12.30. Then visited Barnes[19] to get an exeat from him. Then lunch in rooms. Then visited Wittgenstein: we went off soon together to the Union and fetched some music, thence back to my rooms, where I tried to play it to him! he stayed *chez moi* till about 3.30. Then I packed a few necessaries: we are going up to London for a concert tonight together. I met him at 4.15 outside the Great Gate, and we took a cab to the station. Thence caught the 4.35 GN Ry train to King's Cross. Of course we must needs go first class – very extravagant for me: however he paid for both of us frequently later on and refused to let me repay my share, so I have nothing to complain of. We got out at King's Cross at 6.0 and took a taxi, *via* a shop Wittgenstein wanted to visit, to the Grand Hotel, Trafalgar Square. After obtaining rooms we dined at the Grill room: then took a taxi to the Queen's Hall. The concert began at 8.0: Steinbach conduct-

19 E. W. Barnes (1974–1953), fellow and tutor at Trinity, Pinsent's tutor in Trinity, Bishop of Birmingham 1924–53.

ed and the programme included the Unfinished Symphony, Beethoven's Violin Concerto and Brahms' 1st Symphony. The performance was splendid: I enjoyed the first two items more than ever, and the Brahms (heard for first time) came as a surprise to me, as I had expected not to follow it the first hearing. As a matter of fact I enjoyed it immensely. Afterwards we walked home to the Hotel: Wittgenstein went to bed at once, and I went for a short stroll down to the embankment first.

Tuesday, October 29th, 1912

Breakfast at 7.45. Left in a taxi at 8.15 for Liverpool Street, whence we caught the 8.40 train for Cambridge. Arrived at 10.0, and walked up to Trinity.

Thursday, October 31st, 1912

At 4.30 B. Bell was to have come to tea, but he turned up 3/4 hr late! And immediately after him Winn,[20] and then Wittgenstein appeared (by chance) – and both stayed. B. Bell went early – thank goodness! Winn and Wittgenstein got on better than I should have expected. Winn left about 6.30, but Wittgenstein stayed another hour.

Thursday, November 7th, 1912

At 7.15 I dined at the Union, and went on afterwards to the Guildhall for a recital by Carreño and Backhaus: I had a seat in the 'orchestra'. The programme included a Mozart Sonata for 2 pianos – very fine, some Chopin (played by Carreño) and the 'Appassionata' (played by Backhaus),

[20] Bainbridge-Bell, otherwise unidentified. C. E. Winn (*d.*1973) reading mathematics at Cambridge.

which was terrific and excited me greatly. Got back to my rooms afterwards by 10.0. Soon afterwards Wittgenstein turned up, having also been to the concert, and very enthusiastic about the Mozart. He stayed about an hour.

Friday, November 8th, 1912

Then lunch in rooms. At 2.0 I went *chez* Wittgenstein and then to Couper's, where we got horses for a ride together. We went down to the river and along the tow path to Clay-hithe and back by the Ely road. A tame ride compared with the one I took with Chadwick[21] – as there was no jumping *etc* – but quite pleasant. Wittgenstein was rather depressed at first: he has just heard that his father – who suffers from cancer – has had to be operated on again.

We got back about 4.30 and Wittgenstein came to tea *chez moi*. He stayed till 6.0.

Saturday, November 9th, 1912

Returned to rooms at 6.30 and worked for an hour – interrupted by Wittgenstein who insisted on my dictating him a letter he had to write: he had received an invitation to breakfast and had destroyed the letter before finding out the time and day referred to! So I had to dictate an apologetic reply. Wittgenstein quite frequently gets me to dictate letters like this!

Hall 7.45. Then to the CUMC. They played that Quintet I have been hearing rehearsed, by Dohnányi, very fine indeed. Also Beethoven's 4th Piano and Violin Sonata. Afterwards I went *chez* Wittgenstein – whom I had met at the CUMC. One Farmer* also appeared, a man Witt-

[21] Harold Chadwick, matriculated 1910, later served as a captain in the Royal Army Medical Corps.

genstein dislikes and believes to be dishonest minded:[22] he got very excited trying to induce him to read some good book on some exact science, and see what honest thought is. Which would obviously be good for Farmer – as indeed for any one –: but Wittgenstein was very overbearing and let Farmer know exactly what he thought of him, and altogether talked as if he was his Director of Studies! Farmer took it very well – obviously convinced that Wittgenstein is a lunatic. Farmer, by the way, is a monk – in disguise – though one would never know it from his appearance: he is an undergraduate here, however, doing Moral Sciences – quite young like any other undergraduate. He departed about 11.30; I left at 12.0.

* the man I met *chez* Ponsonby at tea the other day.

Wednesday, November 13th, 1912

At 2.0 I visited Wittgenstein and went with him for a ride (on horseback) along the Huntingdon road, across to Madingley and so home – 9 miles about. It was wet and cold at times – but not bad fun. Got back about 4.0.

Thursday, November 21st, 1912

Then odds and ends till 1.45 when I set out with Wittgenstein to Couper's, where we got horses and went for a ride. We rode along the Trumpington road, through Grantchester, towards Coton and back by the Barton road. The weather was very dull and dark, though it did not actually rain much. Got back 3.45 . . . At 10.0 I went to Russell's squash: only Wittgenstein was there besides myself: we both stayed till 1.0 am – Wittgenstein doing most of the talking.

[22] H. C. M. Farmer, matriculated 1911, killed 1915.

Saturday, November 23rd, 1912

At 4.30 Wittgenstein and Bishop[23] came to tea – the former – from my descriptions of the latter – having desired to meet him. I do not think Wittgenstein was very favourably impressed – Bishop was too lacking in 'go' and enthusiasm for him. Bishop went away early and Wittgenstein stayed till 7.0: I played some Schubert to him, and he got most enthusiastic about it.

Tuesday, November 26th, 1912

At 2.0 I went for a ride with Wittgenstein: the horses were a bit fresh and it was rather fun: we went round by Cherry Hinton. Got back about 4.30 and had tea *chez lui*. Later he came back with me to my rooms, and I played the piano a bit for him – mostly the melodies out of yesterday's concert.

Thursday, November 28th, 1912

At 2.0 I went for a ride with Wittgenstein round by Clayhithe, up by the river and back by the Ely road. It was very cold for one's hands, but otherwise enjoyable. Got back about 4.0. At 4.30 I had tea *chez* Gilson: another man was there, who knew me, though I don't know his name! Came away at 6.0. Later I wrote this diary.

Saturday, November 30th, 1912

Worked from 10 to 12. Then visited Wittgenstein: he made me stay for lunch. Later we went together to Heffers'

[23] J. H. Bishop, matriculated 1911, later served as a lieutenant in the Royal Field Artillery.

(Bookshop) where he had a bill to pay: I bought a cheap edition of Pepys' Diary, and Wittgenstein, apparently struck with the idea, bought a very expensive one! Then we went to the CUMC, and found Lindley there: I talked to him about that Labor[24] Quintet Wittgenstein wants performed, and he said he would try next term: then he and Wittgenstein got arguing about modern music, which was rather amusing. Lindley used not to like modern stuff, but he has been corrupted! These performers always do in the end.

Monday, December 9th, 1912

Went to tea *chez* Wittgenstein at 4.30. Later we went on together to the CUMC – where we performed several songs of Schumann in our usual manner, I at the piano, he whistling.

[24] W. M. Lindley (*d.*1972), matriculated 1910, later served as a captain in the Royal Signals and was awarded the Military Cross and created Chevalier de la Légion d'honneur. Josef Labor (1842–1924), a Bohemian composer and organist, was a *protégé* of the Wittgenstein family.

1913

Monday, January 27th, 1913

About 12.15 pm Wittgenstein suddenly appeared – having only just come up. His father – who has always had cancer – has just died after a longish illness – which is of course what has kept Wittgenstein back.[1] He had lunch *chez moi* and afterwards I went over to his rooms with him and watched him unpacking *etc*. Later Keynes turned up – about 2.30 – I went away about 3.30, leaving Keynes still there – and came back to my room: and wrote this diary *etc*. At 7.0 I went with Wittgenstein and dined at the Union. Thence back to his rooms for a short time, and then he came over with me to my rooms and I played the piano till 10.0 when he went away.

Saturday, February 1st, 1913

Work 11–1. Then had lunch *chez* Wittgenstein: also helped him to sew buttons on to an eiderdown quilt he has

[1] Karl Wittgenstein (1847–1913) died at Vienna on 20 January 1913.

for his bed! Came away at 3.0. At 7.0 I went and dined at the Union and went on afterwards to the CUMC concert. Met Wittgenstein there. The programme included a Brahms Piano Trio and a Bach Concerto for 2 pianos and strings – very good. Back to rooms before 10.0.

Tuesday, February 4th, 1913

Back about 4.0. At 4.30 Butcher and Gilson[2] came to tea. Later – before they left – Wittgenstein also appeared. Quite an entertaining party. Gilson and Butcher went away about 6.0 – Wittgenstein stayed. Then Russell appeared – to inform me of some alterations he is making in the hours of his lectures – and he and Wittgenstein got talking – the latter explaining one of his latest discoveries in the Fundamentals of Logic – a discovery which, I gather, only occurred to him this morning, and which appears to be quite important and was very interesting. Russell acquiesced in what he said without a murmur. Finally they went away together.

Friday, February 7th, 1913

Wittgenstein appeared: he stayed to tea and till 5.30, when I went to Russell's lecture. At 6.30 I went *chez* Wittgenstein and stayed talking till Hall at 7.45. We talked about Woman suffrage: he is very much against it – for no particular reason except that 'all the women he knows are such idiots'. He said that at Manchester University the girl students spend all their time flirting with the professors. Which disgusts him very much – as he dislikes half measures of all sorts, and disapproves of anything not deadly in earnest. Yet in these days, when marriage is not possible till

[2] W. G. D. Butcher, matriculated 1910, killed in 1917 serving as a captain in the London Regiment. R. Q. Gilson, matriculated 1912, killed 1916.

the age of about 30 – no one is earning enough till then – and when illegitimate marriages are not approved of – what else is there to do but to philander?

Saturday, February 8th, 1913

At 2.0 I went for a ride on horses with Wittgenstein. We went out along the Huntingdon road – thence to Madingley – thence to Coton – and home by the Barton road. It was a magnificently sunny afternoon and very enjoyable. Had tea *chez* Wittgenstein when we got home. Went to Russell's lecture from 5.30 to 6.30.

Tuesday, February 11th, 1913

After the concert I went with Wittgenstein up to his rooms. I tried to translate into English a Review he has just written of a book on Logic:[3] he has written the Review in German and gave me a rough translation. But it was very difficult – the construction of the sentences is so different, I suppose, in German to what it is in English. And he insisted on the translation being fairly literal.

Thursday, February 20th, 1913

At 4.45 I went to tea *chez* Wittgenstein. At 6.0 I called on the Junior Proctor... Hall 7.45. Then went with Wittgenstein to a meeting in the Guildhall in support of Woman Suffrage. The speakers were Lord Russell, Mrs Swanwick

[3] P. Coffey, *The Science of Logic* (London: Longmans, Green & Co., 1912). The review appeared in the *Cambridge Review* 34, 6 March 1913, p. 351. The reviewer's verdict is scathing. It ends: 'The worst of such books as this is that they prejudice sensible people against the study of Logic.'

and a Mr Mitchell[4] . . . There were scarcely any militants in the house, except two on the platform, who, when Lord Russell deplored very strongly their tactics, got up and left as a protest.

After the meeting we both went *chez* Russell. Numbers of people turned up later, including Lord Russell, McTaggart[5] and others. They were a very entertaining lot. Lord Russell is very different to his brother, but very pleasant. Came away at 11.45. Wittgenstein came *chez moi* for $\frac{1}{4}$hr before going back to his rooms.

Saturday, February 22nd, 1913

At 2.0 I went for a ride, on horseback, with Wittgenstein. We went out along the Madingley Road. Thence to Madingley by the second turning to the right, thence to the Huntingdon Road and so home. A very good ride with lots of cantering.

Thursday, February 27th, 1913

After changing my clothes, I went *chez* Wittgenstein and found Keynes there: I stayed there about an hour, coming away soon after Keynes left.

Friday, February 28th, 1913

Wittgenstein and Lindley came to tea: there was a lot of animated discussion about modern music – Lindley defending it against us two – which was great fun. Also discussion

4 John Francis Stanley, 2nd Earl Russell (1865–1931), brother of the philosopher. Helena Maria Swanwick (1864–1939), first president of the Women's International League. Mr Mitchell, unidentified.

5 J. M. E. McTaggart (1866–1925), Hegelian philosopher, Fellow of Trinity College, Cambridge, and an Apostle.

about Eugenics and many other topics – in fact quite a successful tea. They both went away about 7.30.

Sunday, March 2nd, 1913

At 7.0 I had dinner with Wittgenstein at the Union. We went on to the Sunday Essay Society (of which I am now a member) at 9.0. Scott (of Clare) read quite a good paper against Moore's 'Principia Ethica'.[6] Moore himself was there and was very amusing afterwards: he admitted the book was all wrong, but not for the reasons given by Scott: he got very earnest and conscientious in discussing the question and climbed all over the sofa, on which he was sitting, in his excitement.

Friday, March 7th, 1913

At 7.30. I went *chez* Wittgenstein to dine with him at the Union: I found him in the middle of a huge discussion with Moore – ramming Russell's Theory of Classes into his (Moore's) head! He went on with his discourse for about 20 minutes after I arrived, when Moore went away. Then we went on to the Union and dined: afterwards Wittgenstein came *chez moi*, and stayed till 9.30 about. We performed all the old Schubert songs, he whistling and I accompanying.

Thursday, March 13th, 1913

. . . caught the 9.25 train to London – arriving Paddington 11.45. Thence took a taxi to Waterloo and deposited luggage at the cloak room there . . . . I went to the National

[6] Sir W. L. Scott (1892–1951), attended Clare College, 1910–13, civil servant. G. E. Moore (1873–1958) was university lecturer in moral science 1911–25. The most influential Apostle of his generation, he was also an active member of the Trinity Sunday Essay Society, to which he had belongad since 1895. His *Principia Ethica* was published in 1903.

Gallery, where I spent about an hour, and then strolled about till 1.45, when I went to the Grill Room of the Grand Hotel, and there met Wittgenstein – by appointment. He is down from Cambridge for the afternoon. We had lunch together there and afterwards took a bus to Townshend and Mercer's shop – in the City – where Wittgenstein bought some porcelain beakers. (He uses them instead of cups in his rooms at Cambridge – because they look so much nicer – but they are less convenient!) Thence we took another bus to Oxford Circus and made a search there for a certain marble masonry: but we found it had been moved to Euston buildings: so we took a taxi thither, and there Wittgenstein ordered a black marble top for a side-board he has at Cambridge: he has hitherto had a white marble top to it. We saw them actually cutting and polishing and carving marble – it was very interesting. Thence we went on in the taxi to the South Kensington Museum, and went over part of the machinery department: Wittgenstein, who of course knows a lot about it, explained it all. We left the Museum about 5.50 and took a taxi back to the Grand Hotel, where we had left our coats. Thence Wittgenstein went on to Liverpool St and so back to Cambridge, and I by tube to Moscow Court.

Saturday, April 12th, 1913

Hall 7.45. Afterwards I picked up Wittgenstein and we went to the CUMC – an 'informal' concert. They did a Chopin Fugue, a Bach Fugue, a movement out of a Brahms' Sonata for Piano and Violin, and a Mozart Trio. Wittengstein came up to my rooms afterwards and stayed till 11.45 pm.

Sunday, April 13th, 1913

Received several letters from Father and Mother, who have just got home. They seem to have had a very successful time. On the journey out – from London to Cologne – they met Wittgenstein, going home to Vienna, and travelled with him. They went to Cologne, Munich, Lago di Garda, Venice, Verona and home by Munich again, dropping Richard there... Went to the Union and had lunch there. Later I went for a walk with Wittgenstein, to Ditton along the river and back by the Newmarket Road.

Thursday, April 17th, 1913

During the morning I did 2 hours work. Lunch in rooms at 12.30. Later I visited Wittgenstein and went with him to the CUMC where we performed several Schubert songs in our usual manner. I returned *chez moi* about 4.0.

Sunday, April 20th, 1913

In the afternoon I went in a canoe on the river with Wittgenstein. We hired the canoe near Trinity College but had it dragged over onto the upper river and eventually went up almost to the University Bathing Place. Got back about 4.15.

Tuesday, April 22nd, 1913

Russell's lecture from 6 to 7. Then went with Wittgenstein and dined with him at the Union. Thence at 8.0. to the Guildhall to a performance of Handel's 'Samson'. A very long thing (though they cut heaps of it) – but in places quite magnificent. It ended at 10.30. Afterwards Wittgenstein came *chez moi* and stayed till 12.0. He told me an excellent story of a Scotch prayer beginning 'Paradoxical as it may seem – oh Lord'!

Wednesday, April 23rd, 1913

At 2.0. I went with Wittgenstein in a canoe on the river – on the backs. Back to rooms about 4.15.

Sunday, April 27th, 1913

About 2.0. I visited Wittgenstein. Later he came to my rooms and we performed some Schubert songs in our customary manner. At 4.30. I had tea with him in his rooms. Muscio also came.[7] We afterwards all three went for a walk – along the river to the Pike and Eel – and back the same way.

Monday, April 28th, 1913

Wittgenstein turned up and stayed till Hall at 7.45. We had a very philosophical argument – on Logic.

Tuesday, April 29th, 1913

From 2 to 3.30. I played tennis with Wittgenstein: he has never played the game before, and I am trying to teach him: so it was a rather slow game!

Wednesday, April 30th, 1913

From 3.30 to 4.30. I played tennis with Wittgenstein: he was much better than yesterday. It drizzled and was very damp. Later I went to tea *chez lui*.

[7] Bernard Muscio, (1887–1928), university demonstrator in Experimental psychology at Cambridge, later professor of philosophy, University of Sidney.

Thursday, May 1st, 1913

I went to the CUMC with Wittgenstein and listened to a rehearsal of the Brahms sextet they did last Saturday.

Saturday, May 3rd, 1913

Wittgenstein appeared at 1.30 – with a proposal that I should go to Spain with him in September: he paying, as last year in Iceland. I have not yet answered definitely, though I should love to go: but what with the Germany scheme with Butcher,[8] it would take up a lot of time, and I shall have to begin reading for the Bar sometime.

Sunday, May 4th, 1913

At 2.0. I went with Wittgenstein in a canoe on the upper river: there was a very strong current flowing. A man in a punt succeeded in absolutely sousing Wittgenstein with water (by mistake!). We landed and Wittgenstein shook his coat violently to dry it, and it was not till we had just re-embarked that he discovered he had shaken out his watch. We searched the place for quite half an hour without success: there was a lot of longish grass, in which the watch must have got concealed.

Monday, May 5th, 1913

At 4.15 I had tea *chez* Wittgenstein, and at 5.0. We went up to the 'New Field' and played tennis. He was off his game

[8] In the summer of 1913 David Pinsent, with his younger brother Richard and his Trinity friend Deane Butcher, went on a walking tour to Bavaria.

today and eventually got sick of it and stopped in the middle of a game.

Tuesday, May 6th, 1913

Went round *chez* Wittgenstein at 10.30 and by taxi with him to the station and thence by the 10.53 to Ely. At the station we met Muscio, who went with us, and also Russell. From Ely station we walked to the Cathedral and heard there a performance of Brahms' 'Requiem'. Quite a fair performance – only their choir and orchestra were not quite large enough for the full effect of the big climaxes. Afterwards we just had time to catch the 1.0. pm train back. From the station at Cambridge Russell biked back, and Wittgenstein, Muscio and I came by bus. Wittgenstein had lunch *chez moi* – about 2.0.

Wednesday, May 7th, 1913

Heard from Mother today, that Wittgenstein's offer is too good to refuse – though of course it will be a very exceptional year in the matter of holidays. So I shall be going both to Germany with Butcher and to Spain with Wittgenstein.

Thursday, May 8th, 1913

From 2 to 3.0. I played tennis with Wittgenstein. He is not getting on very quickly and is getting a bit despondent. At 4.0. I had tea with him in his rooms.

Friday, May 9th, 1913

At 7.15 I dined at the Union, then visited Wittgenstein and with him went to a concert at the Guildhall. The programme was splendid and included Bach's Chaconne, a Mozart Sonata for 2 pianos, the Kreutzer Sonata of Beethoven and Brahms' Variations on a Theme by Haydn. The latter was amazing – the most wonderful thing I had heard for a long while. The theme itself is indescribable – the variations typical of Brahms at his very greatest, and finally when at the end the theme emerges once more, unadorned, fortissimo and in tremendous harmonies, the effect is to make one gasp and grip one's chair! I simply cannot describe how it excited me. After the concert I went *chez* Wittgenstein. Came away and to bed about 11.30.

Sunday, May 11th, 1913

Worked from 12.–1. Then to the Union and lunched there. Then *chez* Wittgenstein and with him for a walk, along the upper river – right bank – by the fields. Got back about 3.45.

Tuesday, May 13th, 1913

Hall 7.45. Then with Wittgenstein to a Union Debate. Hodge* is now president there: his younger brother spoke second tonight and was very futile – though he spoke well. Wittgenstein took a violent dislike to him. We only stayed for 2 speeches, and afterwards I went *chez* Wittgenstein and stayed there till 10.30.

* H. G. Hodge (O.M.)[9]

[9] The abbreviation here stands for Old Marlburian. H. Grose-Hodge (1891–1962) was president of the Union Debating Society, Easter term. He later joined the Indian Civil Service and, subsequently, taught at Charterhouse.

Wednesday, May 14th, 1913

From 3.30. to 4.30. I played tennis with Wittgenstein. I am afraid he is rather hopeless; he is progressing very slowly at the game. Later I went with him for a bike ride – round *via* Girton and Histon.

Thursday, May 15th, 1913

Wittgenstein has been having himself mesmerised – by Dr Rogers here.[10] The idea is this. It is, I believe, true that people are capable of special muscular effort while under hypnotic trance: then why not also special mental effort? So when he (Wittgenstein) is under trance, Rogers is to ask him certain questions about points of Logic, about which Wittgenstein is not yet clear, (– certain uncertainties which no one has yet succeeded in clearing up): and Witt. hopes he will then be able to see clearly. It sounds a wild scheme! Witt. has been twice to be hypnotised – but not until the end of the second interview did Rogers succeed in sending him to sleep: when he did, however, he did it so thoroughly that it took ½ hour to wake him up again completely. Witt. says he was conscious all the time – could hear Rogers talk – but absolutely without will or strength: could not comprehend what was said to him – could exert no muscular effort – felt exactly as if he were under anaesthetic. He felt very drowsy for an hour after he left Rogers. It is altogether a wonderful business. There can be no 'Auto-suggestion' about it – as Wittgenstein once found himself getting drowsy *etc*, when he didn't think Rogers was trying to mesmerise him at all: – just after an attempt had failed, and when he (Witt.) thought the séance was over and was preparing to go away – just talking about other things for a moment before leaving.

[10] Dr Rogers, unidentified.

Friday, May 16th, 1913

At 2.0. I went for a walk with Wittgenstein: on the way we met Russell and he joined us – finally taking us into the Trinity Fellows' Garden.

Saturday, May 24th, 1913

Hall 7.45. Then to the CUMC concert. It was a visit concert – performed by the 'Oxford and Cambridge Musical Club' from London. A very dull programme. I came away with Wittgenstein in the middle, and we went in a canoe on the river for half an hour. Then I came with him to his rooms. Soon afterwards one Mac'Clure[11] turned up – a musical undergraduate – and there was a wild discussion on modern music – Mac'Clure against Witt. and myself. I came away at 12.0 pm.

Wednesday, June 4th, 1913

Did odds and ends till 11.0 – when I went on the river with Wittgenstein in a canoe. We went up to 'the Orchard' at Grantchester, where we had lunch. Wittgenstein was in one of his sulky moods at first, but he woke up suddenly (as always happens with him) after lunch. Then we went on above Byron's pool and there bathed. We had no towels or bathing drawers, but it was great fun. Then we came home again.

Thursday, June 5th, 1913

At 10.15. I went to Russell's squash. Ritchie was there and Muscio. Whitehead[12] turned up later and also Witt-

[11] K. A. J. McClure (*d.*1966), matriculated 1911, later served as a captain in the Middlesex Regiment.

[12] North Whitehead, son of the philosopher A. N. Whitehead.

genstein. I came away at 12.15. After a very amusing evening there, the last of Russell's squashes, I suppose, that I shall go to.

Sunday, June 15th, 1913

Mother and Father and Zelle[13] and Hester all came to tea in my rooms. Then we all went on the upper river, Hester and myself in a canoe and the rest in a rowing boat. We came across Wittgenstein there – in a canoe by himself. Afterwards we all dined at the Union and there met Wittgenstein again and he dined with us.

Monday, June 16th, 1913

At 4.15 pm I returned to the lodgings and we all (Mother, Father, Zelle and Hester and I) went to tea *chez* Wittgenstein. He gave us tea in chemical beakers (as he always has his food – because ordinary crockery is too ugly for him!) – and except that he was somewhat preoccupied by his duties as host was in very good form. At 5.30, Mother and Father and Zelle and Hester went away. I stayed and later went for a walk with Wittgenstein. He proceeded to talk to me about my own character – that I was ideal in all respects, except that he feared that with others except himself I was lacking in generous instincts. He specially said – not with himself – but he feared I did not treat my other friends so generously. By 'generously' he did not imply the ordinary crude meaning – but meant feelings of sympathy *etc.* I don't believe he is right. After all he knows very little of my other friends and my relations with them. And he is so different from other people – he is if anything a bit mad –

[13] Swiss Mademoiselle, governess for Hester, David Pinsent's younger sister.

that one has to deal with him differently – superficially at any rate. He was very nice about it all and spoke in no way that one could resent. When we got back to Trinity St we met Mother *etc* all just returning also, and Witt. was persuaded to dine with us.* He brightened up considerably during dinner and we had a very pleasant evening. Later we all went on the river, Witt. with Hester in a canoe, Zelle and I in a canoe, and Mother and Father in a rowing boat. Afterwards Witt. left us, and I came back to my rooms and played the piano.

* at the lodgings.

Friday, August 22nd, 1913

I heard from Wittgenstein about a month ago, that he would meet me in England, to go to Spain, between Aug. 25th and 30th. But he has written me nothing more definitely since, and I don't know at all where we are to meet. I have written to him to Vienna to London and to Cambridge, but got no answer.

Saturday, August 23rd, 1913

At breakfast I got a long expected letter from Wittgenstein – from Vienna,* that I was to meet him in London on the 30th to start about that date. Just before lunch a telegram arrived from Wittgenstein, from Austria, upsetting everything! He asked if I could meet him at the Grand Hotel in London at 7.30 on Monday the 25th. It was difficult to know if that meant we were to start for Spain about that time, or simply that, knowing (from my letters) that I should be in London about then, he wanted to have a talk with me.

* So the Whiteheads must have been mistaken.

Monday, August 25th, 1913

Thence I caught a train to Waterloo[14] – arriving about 7.20. Thence I took a taxi to the Grand Hotel in Trafalgar Square. I engaged a room for the night and almost at once discovered Wittgenstein in the hall. We proceeded to his bedroom to talk things over, and he told me – firstly that we were not starting till the 30th at the earliest after all. Secondly that he had had influenza – which was why he had been unable to come to England earlier. And thirdly that he had three other alternatives to going to Spain to propose: one, to go to the tiny republic of Andorra – in the Pyrenees and settle there and not travel about as we had intended to do in Spain: two, to go to the Azores, taking a big 'White Star' boat from Malta about Sept. 2nd and returning in a similar sort of boat: and three, to go to Bergen in Norway, and make short walking tours *etc* from there. He was very anxious to shew no preference for any particular scheme and that I should choose unbiased: but it was obvious that his choice was Norway, so eventually I settled on that. I am not sure I shouldn't have preferred the Azores – the voyage would have been very pleasant – but the voyage was precisely what Witt. disliked, as he was sure we should meet crowds of American tourists, which he can't stand! So we are going to Norway and not Spain after all. Why Wittgenstein should have suddenly changed his mind at the last moment I can't think! But I expect it will be great fun in Norway all the same.

About 8.0 we went to the Grill room of the hotel and had dinner. Then we went for a stroll, eventually returning by tube from Westminster about 10.0. Then we went up to his bedroom, and there he explained to me his latest discoveries in Logic. They are truly amazing and have solved all the problems on which he has been working unsatisfactorily for the last year. He always has explained to me what he has been working at,

[14] Pinsent had been staying with his friend Pam and his family in Surbiton.

and it is exceedingly interesting to see how he has gradually developed his work, each idea suggesting a new suggestion, and finally leading to the system he has just discovered – which is wonderfully simple and ingenious and seems to clear up everything. Of course he has upset a lot of Russell's work* – but Russell would be the last to resent that, and really the greatness of his work suffers little thereby – as it is obvious that Wittgenstein is one of Russell's disciples and owes enormously to him. But Wittgenstein's work is really amazing – and I really believe that the mucky morass of Philosophy is at last crystallising about a rigid theory of Logic – the only portion of Philosophy about which there is any possibility of man knowing anything – Metaphysics *etc* are hampered by total lack of data.[§] It is like the transition from Alchemy to Chemistry.

* Russell's work on the fundamental concepts of Logic that is: on his purely Mathematical work – for instance most of his 'Principia' – it has no bearing. Wittgenstein's chief interest is in the very fundamental part of the subject.

§ Really Logic is all Philosophy. All else that is loosely so termed is either Metaphysics – which is hopeless, there being no data – or Natural Science *e.g.* Psychology.

Tuesday, August 26th, 1913

We had breakfast together about 9.30. Afterwards we went out to Cook's and made enquiries about Norway. There is a boat sailing from Hull to Christiania [Oslo] at 6.30 pm next Saturday. If possible we shall catch that and go by train on to Bergen: if not we shall go the whole way by train from Ostende. It depends whether Witt. gets his affairs done in England in time. He has to pay a short visit to Cambridge, to stay a night or so *chez* the Whiteheads near Marlborough, and he wants to see Russell before he starts.

At 11.30 we both went together in a taxi – I with my luggage to Euston, and Witt. thence on to St Pancras – whence he went to Cambridge. I just caught the 11.50 train for Birmingham.

Friday, August 29th, 1913

As soon as I got home I had my luggage put on to the car and after about ten minutes set out myself in the car back to New St Station – to meet Wittgenstein in London and thence to go to Norway. I caught the 2.45 train – and reached Euston without a stop at 4.45. From the station I drove with my luggage in a taxi to the Grand Hotel. Wittgenstein had arranged to meet me there about 5.15 today, but I found no sign of him or message from him. I waited in the Hotel – after engaging a bedroom for the night – till 7.0, and then having left a note for him, should he arrive in my absence, went and had dinner at the Grill room.

I came away before the end of the concert[15] about 10.0 and took a tube back to Trafalgar Square and the hotel. There I found a note from Wittgenstein (he had turned up about 7.30 pm) that he was dining with Russell and had been with him all the afternoon, but would come back to the Hotel about 11.0 pm. He came about 10.30 and took a room for the night close to mine. We sat up in my room till 12.0 talking. It seems that both Russell and old Whitehead are most enthusiastic about his recent work in Logic. It is probable that the first volume of the 'Principia' will have to be re-written, and Wittgenstein may write himself the first eleven chapters. That is a splendid triumph for him!

Saturday, August 30th, 1913

We had breakfast about 9 am. Then we went to Cook's and booked our passages by the Wilson Line S. S. 'Eskimo' – sailing from Hull this evening. They telephoned to Hull to reserve us the necessary accommodation. The ship is due to arrive at Christiania on Monday morning. We were about an hour at Cook's before we got all things settled: afterwards we went by bus to Regent's Park and visited the 'Zoo' – for about

[15] A promenade concert at Queen's Hall.

$\frac{3}{4}$ hour: it was very interesting. We came away from thence about 12.0, and took a bus back to our Hotel. Then we hurriedly packed up everything and at 1.0 pm about set out with our luggage in a taxi for King's Cross. We eventually left by a 1.30 train – in a special through boat-express carriage for Hull. We travelled 1st class. There was a Dining Car on the train, and we had lunch there soon after starting. We had quite a comfortable journey. I slept part of the time and also read a lot of 'Jane Eyre', which I have just begun and am enjoying very much. About 5 pm we got to Doncaster and there both got some tea from the refreshment room, which we took with us into the train and ate as we travelled on. We reached the Quay station at Hull about 6.15, and at once went on board the ship with our luggage. We have got each a two berthed cabin to ourselves – very comfortable. The ship sailed about 6.30 pm.

Soon after we had sailed Wittgenstein suddenly appeared in an awful panic – saying that his portmanteau, with all his manuscripts inside, had been left behind at Hull. In case it might have been put into the hold by mistake we went down thither and searched, but to no effect. Wittgenstein was in an awful state about it. Then, just as I was thinking of sending a wireless message about it, – it was found in the corridor outside someone else's cabin!

About 7. we had dinner down in the saloon. Afterwards we sat on deck together and had a long philosophical discussion about Probability. Later I went inside and wrote a letter home. We both went to bed about 10.30 pm.

This ship is about 3500 tons – about half the size of the boat in which we went to Madeira[16] – but much more comfortable. It has a very roomy smoke room, and a big lounge with a grand piano, and a very roomy top deck.* The sea seems to be absolutely calm – but it is foggy and the hooter is making an awful row every quarter of a minute.

* There are about 40 saloon passengers mostly English.

16 Pinsent had visited the island with his friend Winn between 13 March and 10 April 1913.

Sunday, August 31st, 1913

I got up about 8.0. Wittgenstein – in spite of the sea being absolutely calm – said he felt queer, but he got up and became quite all right soon. We had breakfast in the saloon about 9. Later we paced the deck together for a while. It was still quite calm but foggy, and the hooter was still going – as it had been all night. It remained foggy almost all day – though occasionally for a short time the fog lifted and we could go on quicker. Later I went inside and wrote this Diary. Lunch in the saloon was at 1.30 pm. During the rest of the day I sat and read 'Jane Eyre' and did odds and ends. I had some tea on deck about 4.30. Dinner in the saloon at 7.0. About 9.0 there were lighthouses visible on the port side. I went to bed about 11.0. During the night we called at Christiansand in Norway, but we did not stay there long and were off again long before I got up next morning.

Monday, September 1st, 1913

We both had breakfast in the saloon at 9.0 am. We were due to reach Christiania this morning at 8 am, but the fog has delayed us a lot. It was still foggy on and off last night, and is still so this morning. Occasionally it cleared and one saw land to port. During the morning I read and paced the deck with Wittgenstein. Lunch at 1.30 as usual. Afterwards we found ourselves in the Fjord nearing Christiania: the fog had cleared and it was very beautiful. There were lots of sailing boats about and I explained to Wittgenstein all about their rig and difference *etc.*[17] We got to the quay at Christiania about 4.30. By this time it had begun to rain – though it had been sunny except for the fog all the voyage so far. We got our luggage off and passed it through the customs: they made us open everything, but did not make a

[17] Pinsent had sailed frequently on family holidays in Castle Townshend, Ireland, and Falmouth.

very strict examination and passed it all through. Then we drove with it in a cab to the Grand Hotel – and engaged two single rooms for the night. Later we went out to the Post office and left instructions for letters (sent Poste Restante thither) to be forwarded. We came back to the Hotel and had dinner about 7.30. Went to bed about 10.0 pm.

I may as well mention here that Wittgenstein is paying my expenses on this tour exactly as he did last year in Iceland. We are not taking so much money with us this time, however, as last year. We have about £70 between us, which we have shared. And Wittgenstein has also a letter of Credit to draw upon.

Tuesday, September 2nd, 1913

Got up at 6. am, packed, and had breakfast at 6.30. After paying the bill *etc* we set out in a taxi to the station about 7.0. We registered our luggage to Bergen and eventually caught the train thither at 7.35 am. We travelled 2nd class (there are no 1sts on this line).

Last night and this morning there was a terrific business between me and Wittgenstein – but thank goodness it is now completely reconciled. It began yesterday evening. We had got on splendidly up till then and he was saying as much – that we 'had got on splendidly so far, hadn't we?' I always find it exceedingly hard to respond to his fervent outbursts, and I suppose this time I instinctively tried to turn it off flippantly – I am horribly shy of enthusiasm about that sort of thing. But I somehow offended him and he said not a word more that evening. This morning he was absolutely sulky and snappish – but till we got into the train we were very much hurried and had lots to do. On the train we had to change our seats at the last moment because he insisted on being alone from other tourists. Then a very genial Englishman came along and talked to me and finally insisted on our coming into his carriage to smoke – as ours was a non-smoker. Witt. refused to move, and of course I had to go for a short time at least – it would have been violently rude to refuse. I came back as soon as I could and found him in an awful state. I made some remark about the Englishman being a weird person – whereat he turned and said 'I could travel the whole way with him if I pleased'. And then I had it all out with him and finally brought him round to a normal and genial frame of mind. I had been meaning to have it out all the morning – I can always reconcile things with him when I get a chance of being frank and open – but one trivial circumstance after another had made it impossible. When I did get the opportunity, we made it up in ten minutes. He is a chaotic person. I have to be frightfully careful and tolerant when he gets these sulky fits. He is – in his acute sensitiveness – very like Levin in 'Anna Karenina', and thinks the most awful things of me when he is sulky – but is very contrite afterwards. The only other person in the world whom he knows as intimately as me – is Russell: and he has the same scenes periodically with Russell. I know that both from Russell and himself.

About 9 we went along to a restaurant car on the train and had a second breakfast. We were the whole day in the train – and it was the most wonderful railway journey I have ever made. The total distance is about 320 miles, and the train went along seldom over 30 miles an hour – taking 14 hours altogether stopping frequently for about 10 minutes when the passengers all got out and walked about. For the first 8 hours we went steadily up – along valleys – finally reaching a height of almost 4,500 ft and then steadily down to Bergen. Down in the valleys the country is very wooded, but up higher there is only grass, and higher still nothing but rock and glacier – quite arctic. Up high the line is protected against snow drifts (in winter) by high pallisades made of wood. They don't obscure one's view so very much however, as they are built a fair way from the line on either side. At some places, however, the line goes through a complete artificial tunnel of wood. There are an enormous number of tunnels all the way. The views, especially at the Bergen end, are magnificent. It was a glorious sunny day – which made them all the finer. Up at the top at midday it was chilly – but the sun was strong – like in Switzerland in winter. Down on the sea level, however, it is quite warm and mild.

We had lunch in the dining car at 2.0 pm. Also some tea about 6.0 and supper at 7.30 pm. Afterwards I had a conversation with Wittgenstein about how we got on together *etc*. These sulky fits of his, I am afraid, distress him very much. He is very anxious that we should have less friction this time than last year in Iceland. I thought we got on very well last year considering – but our occasional rows – when he was fussy or I irritated by some trivial detail – seem to have distressed him a lot. He says that at times last year he was even uncertain whether to like or dislike me* – but that since then we have got to know each other much better and he is never uncertain now. I am afraid he is in an even more sensitive neurotic state just now than usual, and it will be very hard to avoid friction altogether. We can always avoid it at Cambridge, when we don't see so much of each other: but he never will understand that it becomes infinitely harder when we are together so much as now: and it puzzles him frightfully.

We reached Bergen at 9.15 pm, and drove from the station in the hotel bus to the Hotel Norge. There we got two single rooms for the night. Later we went out for a short stroll, and soon afterwards went to bed.

* Also that he enjoyed the Iceland trip 'as much as it is possible for two people to do, who are nothing to each other'. I certainly enjoyed it more than that.

Wednesday, September 3rd, 1913

We had breakfast about 9.30 am. Afterwards we went out to Beyer's Tourist Office to make enquiries. We want a small place – where there is a small hotel – somewhere on a Fjord, amongst pleasant country – and where we can be quite alone from Tourists (upon this Ludwig is very firm).

We want to settle down in such a place for say 3 weeks – and do some work (I at Law and Ludwig at Logic) – and get some walking and sailing on the Fjord also if possible. I really think we shall get such a place – but we arranged to call later (at Beyer's,) when they had made enquiries. Then we returned to the Hotel and sat up in my room for about 1½hrs – I writing my Diary – and Ludwig working. When he is working he mutters to himself* and strides up and down the room all the while. At 1.30 – we went again to Beyer's. They suggested three places – of which the best seemed Öistesö[18] – a small village on the Hardanger Fjord – where there is a small hotel. They tried to telephone, while we were there, and ask about terms and accommodation – but could not get through, as the line was closed till 4 pm. So we arranged to call again about 5.15. We returned to the Hotel and had lunch at 2.0. Afterwards we went for a drive in an open 'victoria' – it was fine and sunny up a hill behind the town. The views were splendid. We had some tea at a restaurant half way up the hill, and then drove down again – finally ending at Beyer's about 5.15. Then they telephoned to Öistesö and heard that we could get the accommodation we wanted – also that there were a few people staying there, but they would be gone soon. So we settled to go there and got tickets by steamer thither for tomorrow. Later we did a lot of shopping and odds and ends and finally returned to the Hotel for supper at 8.0. Later we went for a short stroll and also I strummed on a piano in the Hotel. To bed about 10.30 pm.

* in a mixture of German and English.

Thursday, September 4th, 1913

We got up at 6.30 am – had breakfast at 7.15 – and after paying the bill *etc* – set out in a cab to the quay whence the steamer for Öistesö started. Our luggage went separately on

[18] The name of the place today is *Öystese*. The spelling 'Öistesö' was current at the time of Pinsent's and Wittgenstein's visit.

a barrow. We went on board the steamer – a small one such as one finds on Swiss lakes *etc* – and it started at 8.0 am. We had a second breakfast on board about 8.30. The boat went along channels between the islands all the way and the views were very nice – it was fine and sunny. We had lunch on board about 2.0 pm. We called at several places on the way, finally reaching Öistesö about 6 pm. During a lot of the journey I slept. We got off at Öistesö and the Hotel landlord met us and conducted us to the Hotel just close by. He is a quiet man – very pleasant.* At the hotel we got two single bed rooms and another big room, which they converted into a Private sitting room for us. They all look out onto the Fjord – a perfectly splendid view. Öistesö is a tiny village in a little bay of the Fjord with hills rising straight behind. It seems the ideal place we want.

Later we went out for a stroll. I took my camera with me – which was the cause of another scene with Ludwig. We were getting on perfectly amicably – when I left him for a moment to take a photo. And when I overtook him again he was silent and sulky. I walked on with him in silence for half an hour, and then asked him what was the matter. It seemed, my keenness to take that photo had disgusted him – 'like a man who can think of nothing – when walking – but how the country would do for a golf course'. I had a long talk with him about it, and eventually we made it up again. He is really in an awful neurotic state: this evening he blamed himself violently and expressed the most piteous disgust with himself. At first I was rather annoyed with him – it seemed to me that his feelings were silly and rather selfish. But afterwards I could only pity him – it is obvious he is quite incapable of helping these fits. I only hope that an out of doors life here will make him better: at present it is no exaggeration to say he is as bad – (in that nervous sensibility) – as people like Beethoven were. He even talks of having at times contemplated suicide.

When we got back to the Hotel we had supper (at 8 pm). There we encountered the other occupants of the hotel: there are about 10 besides ourselves – all of them Norwegians, except one married couple of whom I am not sure:

I rather think the wife is English and the husband Norwegian: they usually speak Norwegian. After supper we went for a stroll, and later came back to the hotel and sat in our sitting room and played Dominoes – (we had bought a set in Bergen). To bed about 10.30 pm.

* He speaks very good English.

Friday, September 5th, 1913

We had breakfast at 9 am. Afterwards I wrote a lot of this diary. We had asked our hotel manager if we could hire a small sailing boat here, and during this morning he found one for us and I went and inspected it. It was an open boat – about 18ft long – with no keel or centre-board – and rigged with a foresail and mainsail (the latter very primitive, with no boom or gaff, but a spar going diagonally from the bottom of the mast). We agreed to hire it permanently, while we were here, at the very cheap rate of 1 Krone a day. Later we took some lunch with us from the hotel and went out in it. But we could not go far as there was very little wind.* We had lunch on board – drifting about meanwhile. I managed the sailing myself – as Ludwig knows nothing about it.§ We came ashore again about 2.30 pm. Later I wrote this diary – and later played on a piano there is in this hotel. About 6 pm we went for a stroll together along the shore. We returned to the hotel for supper at 8.0. In the evening we went for a short stroll and later played dominoes as yesterday.

* It was a fine – sunny day.

§ We have the boat entirely to ourselves – no paid hand with us to help.

Saturday, September 6th, 1913

We had breakfast at 9.30. During the morning I wrote this diary *etc* and Ludwig worked. About 1.0 we took lunch with us and walked up to a little lake in the hills behind – about an hour's walk. It was fine and sunny and the view by the lake quite gorgeous. We had lunch near the lake and afterwards walked down again to the hotel. Then we went out in our sailing boat: there was very little wind, but more than yesterday. We came back to the hotel abut 5.30, and had some tea. Afterwards Witt. worked and I did odds and ends. After supper at 8.0 we went for a short stroll together and then came home and played Dominoes. To bed about 11.0 pm.

Sunday, September 7th, 1913

Breakfast at 9.15 about. Afterwards I wrote this diary. About 12.0 we went out in our sailing boat. There was more wind than we have had so far – but still not much. And it was very variable and came only in occasional puffs. We came ashore again about 1.45 – and had lunch at the Hotel. Afterwards we went out again in the boat: this time we rowed her a good way out* – further than we have ever got so far – and there found quite a lot of wind and had a very good sail. We had to row home again however, as there was never much wind inside. We got back ashore about 7.0. I did about 1/2 hrs work at Law between then and supper at 8. After supper we went for a short stroll and then played dominoes as usual. We always begin by playing proper dominoes, and end by building wonderful systems with the domino-pieces – with ingenious arrangements for knocking them down – also constructed out of domino pieces!

* Hitherto we had always tried to sail out – but never got very far.

Monday, September 8th, 1913

Breakfast at 9.30. Later I wrote this diary. The weather – having been fine and cloudless right up till yesterday evening – has broken and it is now cloudy though not actually raining. Later in the morning I did a lot of work at Law. Ludwig also worked. We had lunch – at the hotel – at 2.0 pm. In the afternoon we went for a walk to Nordheimsund and back – about 4 miles each way. It rained a good deal, but we wore overcoats, so did not get very wet. We walked thither by the coast road and back over the hills. At Nordheimsund we went to the Hotel and had some tea. During a lot of the time we talked about Logic – about the 'Theory of Types' – upon which Wittgenstein is now working. We got back to our hotel at Öistesö at 8.0, and had supper as soon as we got in. Later we played dominoes as usual.

Tuesday, September 9th, 1913

At breakfast I received two letters from Mother – one forwarded from Poste Restante Christiania and again from the hotel at Bergen, and the other forwarded from Poste Restante Bergen. In the morning I wrote this diary. I also did a lot of work at Law. Ludwig also worked. About 12.30 we took lunch with us and set out sailing in our little boat for an island just at the mouth of the bay of Öistesö. We had to beat out all the way against the wind. Today there was quite a fair breeze, but we took some time getting there, as the direct distance was quite 3½ miles. We got to the island and landed there about 3.15 pm – and then had our lunch upon it. The weather was fairly fine – sunny at times and no rain. We set out home again about 4.0, and then found that the wind had changed right round, so that we had to beat all the way again. However there was still quite a fair lot of wind and we got home by 6.30 pm. Our little boat is somewhat clumsy – very slow in the stays – and carries an appalling lot of lee-helm: she won't sail very close to the wind: but we get on with her very well considering. Distances here look so much less than they really are, so that one seems to be going much slower than one is really. We had tea in the hotel when we got back. Later I did about half an hour's Law. Supper as usual at 8.0. Afterwards we went for a short stroll and then back to the hotel and played dominoes as usual.

Wednesday, September 10th, 1913

I got up at 8 am, and went for a walk along the shore, before breakfast, by myself: I took my camera and took two photos: On my way back I was suddenly attacked by a small dog – who tried to bite me in the leg. I had done nothing to him – and only realised his existence when I suddenly found him biting me! He only tore my trousers, however, and did not hurt my leg a bit! I got back to the hotel and had breakfast with Ludwig about 10.0. From 10.30 till 2.0 I worked at Law – Ludwig also worked. Then we had lunch in the hotel. Afterwards we went for a walk: the weather had been sunny in the morning, but later it clouded over though it did not rain. We scrambled some way up along the bed of a stream – jumping from rock to rock – the water flowed amongst hosts of boulders. Ludwig was very clumsy and fell into the water several times and got very wet: however it was great fun. We came home by 5.30, and had tea in the hotel. Later I did some work at Law and also strummed on the piano. Supper at 8. Later we went for a stroll and afterwards played dominoes as usual.

Thursday, September 11th, 1913

We had breakfast about 9.45 am. It was a wet and drizzly and misty day. After breakfast Ludwig suddenly decided to leave me for two days here, and go to Bergen, where he wants to buy several things, which can't be obtained in the few shops here.* He decided to leave by a 12.30 steamer this morning, arriving Bergen at 8. this evening: to sleep tonight in Bergen, and start back by a 4 pm steamer from Bergen tomorrow – sleeping on board and arriving back here at 11 am on Saturday. We spent most of the morning thinking out and making a list of everything he is to do in Bergen. The steamer was very late and did not leave till 1.30. I saw him off from the quay. I had lunch in the hotel at 2.0 pm. Later I did a lot of work at Roman Law. I had some tea about 5 and later played the piano a good deal. Later I converted my bedroom into a dark room and made all preparations for developing after supper. I had supper at 8. All the original visitors to the hotel (besides ourselves) are now gone: there have been occasional new visitors, mostly commercial travellers staying for one night – but at the present moment there is nobody but myself. After supper I developed one spool of six films: they were all quite good: one of them was taken at Hirnsbirg in Bavaria, but the other 5 in Norway. I washed them and hung them to dry before going to bed.

* It is a nuisance, our having to separate: but we are very much in need of the things Ludwig is going to buy, and there would be no point in our both going.

Friday, September 12th, 1913

Got up and had breakfast by 8.45. Afterwards I wrote this diary. Later I went for a walk by myself. It was a cloudy day and very apt to rain. It was not raining when I set out, but started to before I got back, and I had to change all my clothes when I got in. Afterwards I worked at Law till lunch at 2.0 – and again after lunch till 4.30 about, when I had some tea. Later I played the piano a bit. Afterwards I borrowed a little rowing boat, belonging to the hotel, and went for a row on the Fjord. It was very squally – and therefore impossible to sail – and the water quite rough. I came in and had supper about 8. Later I did odds and ends and went to bed about 10.30.

Saturday, September 13th, 1913

After breakfast I worked at Law, till 11.0 when I met the steamer from Bergen and Ludwig. He had bought all the things we wanted, and also two volumes of Schubert's songs. Later we performed some of these in our customary manner. At 2.0 we had lunch in the hotel. During the afternoon we did odds and ends and performed more Schubert. We had tea in the hotel at 4.30 about. Later we went for a walk* – along the coast road in the opposite direction from Nordheimsund. We got back about 8 for supper. Later we played dominoes as usual.

We are now quite alone in the hotel except for the Hotel proprietor and his wife (and the servants *etc*). The hotel man and his wife are both very pleasant people. They have lived for 19 years in Chicago in America, and speak very good English with a strong American accent.

* It was a cloudy, stormy day – but not much rain.

Sunday, September 14th, 1913

We had breakfast about 9.45 am. Later we made a terrific fuss trying to destroy a wasp's nest. Twice yesterday I had a wasp crawl up my trouser leg: once I was stung, and the other time shook it out before it could sting. This morning we searched for the nest, and soon found it – in the roof of a balcony there is in the ground floor of the hotel. We tried to stuff up the entrance with cotton wool, soaked in petroleum and methylated spirits. I don't know how far we succeeded – there were still lots of wasps buzzing round it when we left it. Later I wrote a letter home and worked at Law. We had lunch in the hotel at 2.0. In the afternoon we went for a walk to Porsmyr and back – about 4 miles each way. It was fine and sunny and the views magnificent. Porsmyr is on a long narrow inlet of the Hardanger-fjord –

with high precipitous mountains on either side. We got back to the hotel at Öistesö about 7. Supper at 8. Later we performed some Schubert and afterwards played dominoes.

Monday, September 15th, 1913

After breakfast we made a second onslaught on the wasps' nest. We succeeded, after a great fuss, in getting some benzine in the village – and tried to pour it into the nest. But it wasn't much of a success, we ought to have had a squirt, but couldn't get one. Later I worked at Law and also played the piano a lot. Had lunch in the hotel at 2.0. In the afternoon Ludwig stayed in and worked: I went for a walk by myself – up to the lake we went to on Saturday the 6th – and back. It was gloriously fine and sunny. I got back about 5 and we both had tea together in the hotel. Did odds and ends till supper at 8. Later we went for a stroll and afterwards played dominoes.

Tuesday, September 16th, 1913

At breakfast I got a post card from Mother, and later in the day a letter from her – enclosing two letters sent to me to Lordswood – one from Winn, and one from Estelle King,[19] about the next meeting of 'the Club'. That next meeting is going to be inexpressibly edifying! Most unfortunately I shall not be returned to England in time for it. They are going to 'take the 17th century and look up the different aspects – each person taking some different subject'. And it is suggested that I should give them a discourse on the Astronomy or the Mathematics of the period.

During the morning I wrote this diary. Later I played the piano a lot. We had lunch in the hotel at 2.0. Afterwards I

[19] A Birmingham acquaintance who ran a play reading group.

made my bedroom into a dark room and made preparations for developing. We had tea about 5.0, and then I developed a spool of six photos., I have taken here during the last few days. They were all quite good. Later – about 7 pm – Ludwig and I went for a stroll.* We returned to the hotel for supper at 8.0. Afterwards we played dominoes *etc* as usual.

* It was a fine sunny day.

Wednesday, September 17th, 1913

During the morning I wrote sundry letters – to Mother and Winn and Estelle. I also played the piano. We had lunch in the hotel about 2.0 pm. During all the morning and most of the afternoon Ludwig was very gloomy and unapproachable – and worked at Logic all the time. He had been quite cheerful of late up till today. In the afternoon I went for a walk by myself – some way up the hills behind Öistesö and back. I got home at about 5 – and had tea with Ludwig at the hotel. Then I somehow succeeded in cheering him up – back to his normal frame of mind – and after tea we went for a stroll together (it was a fine sunny day). We got talking and it appeared that it had been some very serious difficulty with the 'Theory of Types' that had depressed him all today. He is morbidly afraid he may die before he has put the Theory of Types to rights, and before he has written out all his other work in such a way as shall be intelligible to the world and of some use to the science of Logic. He has written a lot already – and Russell has promised to publish his work if he were to die – but he is sure that what he has already written is not sufficiently well put, so as absolutely to make plain his real methods of thought *etc* – which of course are of more value than his definite results. He is always saying that he is certain he will die within four years – but today it was two months.

We got back to the hotel about 8, and had supper. Later we performed a lot of Schubert and afterwards played dominoes as usual.

Thursday, September 18th, 1913

After breakfast I wrote this diary. I also played the piano a lot. We had lunch in the hotel at 2.0. Afterwards we performed a lot of Schubert. About 4.30 we set out driving to Nordheimsund; in a queer two wheeled vehicle we hired in the village – an open one with seats for two in front – and a little seat behind for the driver. It was a cloudy day and rained a little but we took our oilskins and did not get wet. The drive – by the coast road both ways – was very enjoyable. At Nordheimsund we went to the hotel and had some tea: we also did a little shopping there. We got back to the hotel at Öistesö about 6.30, and then made another onslaught on the old wasps' nest – having bought some benzine and a squirt in Nordheimsund. This time I really think we did get the benzine into the nest and kill some of the wasps. We had supper at 8, and afterwards came out to look at the wasps' nest, and found the ground all round swarming with half stupefied crawling wasps – which we killed by dozens. They were huge and enormous wasps and terrifying to watch. I suppose they were some who had managed to crawl out of the nest in spite of the benzine: I hope the others – who could not crawl out – are all dead. Later we performed some Schubert and then played dominoes and then to bed.

Friday, September 19th, 1913

During the morning I worked a lot at Roman Law, and also played the piano. We had lunch in the hotel at 2.0. During the afternoon I sat out in front of the hotel – (it was fine and sunny) – and read 'Daniel Deronda' (by George Eliot) which I have just begun. I have just finished 'Jane Eyre' – having enjoyed it very much. I don't know that it is a very great work – it is apt at times to be crude and unconvincing – but still it is very good. I had tea in the hotel with Ludwig about 5. Later we went for a stroll together. The fjord looked perfectly wonderful in the evening light tonight. We got back to the the hotel for supper at 8. Afterwards we performed some Schubert and later played dominoes as usual.

Saturday, September 20th, 1913

During the morning I did a lot of work at Roman Law – and played the piano. We had lunch in the hotel at 2.0. Afterwards I sat out in front of the hotel and read 'Daniel Deronda' till about 5.0, when I had tea with Ludwig. We afterwards went for a stroll together (it was fine mostly – with occasional showers). Ludwig was horribly depressed all this evening. He has been working terribly hard of late – which may be the cause of it. He talked again tonight about his death – that he was not really afraid to die – but yet frightfully worried not to let the few remaining moments of his life be wasted. It all hangs on his absolutely morbid and mad conviction that he is going to die soon – there is no obvious reason that I can see why he should not live yet for a long time. But it is no use trying to dispel that conviction, or his worries about it, by reason: the conviction and the worry he can't help – for he is mad. It is a hopelessly pathetic business – he is clearly having a miserable time of it. This evening too he was worried horribly that perhaps after all his work in Logic was no real use: and then his nervous temperament had caused him a life of misery and others considerable inconvenience – all for nothing. I tried to convince him that his work could not be entirely useless – that it was impossible yet for anyone to judge exactly about it, least of all himself. I think I succeeded partially – he went to bed fairly cheerful.

We had supper in the hotel at 8.0. We played dominoes afterwards as usual.

Sunday, September 21st, 1913

After breakfast I wrote this diary. Later I worked at Law, and also played the piano. We had lunch at 2.0.

Afterwards we performed some Schubert – and later I did more work at Law. We had tea in the hotel about 5.0. Afterwards we took our sailing boat – with the mast and rigging taken out – and rowed out to the island at the mouth of the bay of Öistesö (which we visited once before) and back.* I rowed all of both ways. We had not started for long, however, before we discovered that the boat was leaking violently. But we managed to keep her moderately dry till we got to the island by Ludwig bailing occasionally. At the island we landed and searched the boat for the leak and eventually found that the plug had come out of the small hole which is made in the bottom of every boat. We stuffed up the hole with Ludwig's handkerchief – bailed all the water out – and rowed home quite dry. We got back about 8. and had supper when we got in. Later we performed some Schubert and played dominoes as usual. We have now a repertoire of some 40 Schubert songs – which we perform – Ludwig whistling the air and I playing the accompaniment.

* There was no wind at all for sailing, but it was a fine sunny day.

Monday, September 22nd, 1913

During the morning I worked a lot at Law – and played the piano. We had lunch at 2.0. Afterwards we performed some Schubert and later I did more Law. We had tea in the hotel about 5.30. Afterwards we went for a walk together – up to the woods and back on the non-coast road to Nordheimsund. We came back to the hotel for supper at 8. Afterwards we performed Schubert and played dominoes. It was a fine, sunny day.

Tuesday, September 23rd, 1913

During the morning I worked at Law and later played the piano. Later I went for a short stroll with Ludwig – it was a fine, sunny day. We had lunch in the hotel at 2.0. Afterwards we performed some Schubert, and at about 4.15 took our sailing boat – without the mast and rigging – and rowed out to a large island just beyond the one we have visited twice before – and back. We took two pairs of oars with us this time (hitherto we have only taken one pair) – and I rowed both ways and Ludwig also rowed with me for part of the way back. We landed on the island about 5.15 – and fooled about there till 6.20 or so – when we started home again. Whilst we were on the island we had a long conversation about this holiday and holidays in general. Ludwig says he has never before enjoyed a holiday so much as this. He is almost certainly speaking the truth – but it is curious, considering how depressed he has been at times lately: but I suppose these fits of depression are always with him and nothing exceptional. He has certainly been very cheerful indeed when he has not been depressed. As regards myself I am enjoying myself pretty fairly – there is just enough to do to keep one from being bored. But living with Ludwig alone in his present neurotic state is trying at times – though when he is nice he is charming.

We got back to the hotel about 7.30 – and had supper at 8. Later we played dominoes. This evening I got a letter from Mother – with one enclosed from Hester.

Ludwig and I have had no other rows but the two occasions I mentioned. I have been all the time very much on the look out, and have had to take care always in order to avoid friction. It is this which makes it so trying at times to live alone with Ludwig. But all the same there is not much to complain of – as he is a very charming companion so long as friction is avoided.

Wednesday, September 24th, 1913

During the morning I wrote a letter home. I also did some work at Law. Ludwig was very cheerful this morning, but suddenly announced a scheme of the most alarming nature. To wit. that he should exile himself and live for some years right away from everybody he knows – say in Norway. That he should live entirely alone and by himself – a hermit's life – and do nothing but work in Logic. His reasons for this are very queer to me – but no doubt they are very real for him: firstly he thinks he will do infinitely more and better work in such circumstances, than at Cambridge, where, he says, his constant liability to interruption and distractions (such as concerts) is an awful hindrance. Secondly he feels that he has no right to live in an antipathetic world (and of course to him very few people are sympathetic) – a world where he perpetually finds himself feeling contempt for others, and irritating others by his nervous temperament – without some justification for that contempt *etc*, such as being a really great man and having done really great work. The first of the above reasons I cannot understand – I should go wild with boredom if I lived alone, and be unable to do any work without some distraction. But I believe he really is different and could easily stand it. The second reason above I consider quite Quixotic: but he feels it very strongly all the same. He has not definitely made up his mind – but there is great probability of his adopting the scheme eventually.

We had lunch at the hotel at 2.0. Later we performed some Schubert. Later I did more work at Law. We had tea about 5.30. Afterwards we went for a stroll together – it was fine and sunny. We came back for supper at 8. Later we performed some Schubert and played dominoes as usual.

This afternoon I was again stung by a wasp crawling up my leg!

Thursday, September 25th, 1913

After breakfast I wrote this diary. During the morning also I did a little packing – some Law – and helped Ludwig with a paper he has just begun writing for the Working Men's College in London, on philosophy. It is the introductory lecture of a course he is to give there on philosophy.[20] We had lunch at 2.0. Afterwards we did some Schubert and also more of the paper on philosophy. We had tea at 6.0. Afterwards we went for a stroll together, returning to the hotel for supper at 8 – it was a fine day. Later we did more Schubert and played dominoes as usual.

This evening we got talking together about suicide – not that Ludwig was depressed or anything of the sort – he was quite cheerful all today. But he told me that all his life there had hardly been a day, in which he had not at one time or other thought of suicide as a possibility. He was really surprised when I said I never thought of suicide like that – and that given the chance I would not mind living my life so far – over again! He would not for anything.

Friday, September 26th, 1913

During the morning I packed – did odds and ends – and played the piano. We had lunch at the hotel at 2.0. Afterwards I read some of 'Daniel Deronda', and again played the piano. We had tea about 5.0. In the afternoon I received a letter from Mother. After tea Ludwig and I went for a stroll together: it was a cloudy day and apt to rain, but did not rain just while we went out now. We came back to the hotel about 7.0, and then Ludwig packed – I helping him – getting it done by 8 – when we had supper. After supper we paid the bill *etc* for our three weeks stay here. We also did some Schubert and played dominoes till 10.30 pm. At 11.0 we set out driving to Nordheimsund. There was no convenient steamer calling at Öistesö – so we had to catch one from Nordheimsund. We drove in the same open trap we had last time we drove to Nordheimsund, and our luggage came in a cart with us. It was raining hard when we set out, but we had

[20] See the entry for 29 September below and see also Brian McGuinness, *Wittgenstein, A life: Young Ludwig (1889–1921)*, ch. 5, p. 170.

our coats and an umbrella borrowed from the hotel. It was pitch dark and rather enjoyable driving. We reached Nordheimsund about 11.45 – and sheltered from the rain in the porch of the Hotel there. Later the landlady came out and asked us if we would come and wait inside – which we very gladly did. The steamer was due to arrive at 12.0, but did not come till half an hour later. At last – from inside the hotel – we heard its approaching hoot – and went out and soon got on board with our luggage. We got a two berthed cabin for ourselves – we tried to get two separate cabins, but couldn't, and went to bed almost at once.

Saturday, September 27th, 1913

The steamer got to the quay at Bergen at 8 in the morning. We both got up by then – and having got the captain of the steamer to telephone for us for a cab – drove in it with our luggage to the Hotel Norge. There we had breakfast at once – and engaged two single rooms. Later we went out and did a lot of odds and ends and shopping. We came back to the hotel about 11.0, and for the rest of the morning I sat and read. We had lunch at 2.0. During the afternoon I went for a short stroll by myself and later another stroll with Ludwig. We had supper at 8.0. Afterwards I read. Went to bed about 9.30. It was a drizzly misty day.

Sunday, September 28th, 1913

We had breakfast at 9.45 am about. During the morning I played a little on a piano in the Hotel, and later wrote this diary, I also went for a short stroll with Ludwig – between 1 and 2 pm. Had lunch at the hotel at 2. Afterwards at 3.15 I set out for a walk by myself. It was a glorious fine and sunny day. I went along the shore (leaving Bergen to the left – facing the sea) to a village about 3½ miles off – thence back by another road going up high on the face of the hill behind – and finally down again to Bergen. I got back to the Hotel Norge about 6 – after having had some tea at a restaurant on the way. Later I played the piano a bit. Later I went for a short stroll with Ludwig. We had supper at the hotel at 8. Afterwards we played dominoes.

Monday, September 29th, 1913

After breakfast we went out and did some shopping *etc*. We came back to the hotel – got everything packed *etc* by 11.45 – to go aboard the steamer for Newcastle. At the last moment a rug of Ludwig's was found missing – but it was eventually found after a lot of fuss. Someone else* had carried it off to another hotel (whence it was now fetched) presumably under the impression it was his. We drove in a cab to the quay and got on board the S. S. 'Vega' by about 12.30 pm. The ship sailed about 1.15. Just after that we had a great fuss about cabins: we could not get two separate cabins as the boat was full – and had to occupy a 2-berthed cabin. We had lunch in the saloon about 2.30 pm.

All today the ship went in sheltered waters – between islands. The views were very fine – it being a fine sunny day. In the afternoon Ludwig and I wrote his paper for the Working Men's College§ a lot – from 3 to 5 about. Later we paced the deck a lot – and also made a visit to the engine rooms – which were interesting but greasy. At about 6.30 we called at a place, whose name I can't remember. We only made about 5 minutes halt there – did not even anchor or moor at a quay – taking on and putting off a few passengers and mails in a small boat. Soon after this we had supper in the saloon – at 8.0. We got to Stavanger about 9.0, and moored to a quay there. Soon after we arrived Ludwig and I went ashore and strolled about the town. We came back on board about 10.15 pm. The ship left Stavanger about 11.0. There was quite a crowd on shore and on board waving 'Good-bye' as we steamed away – and not only waving, but they all sang a curious sort of chant as we gradually receded. We went to bed soon after starting.

* who had been staying at the Hotel Norge – but moved off to another hotel.

§ The paper was afterwards abandoned – unfinished – owing to Ludwig's decision to live in Norway.

Tuesday, September 30th, 1913

Got up about 8.0 and found ourselves in the open North Sea. The ship rolled and pitched a bit all day – but it was not really very rough. It was perfectly fine and sunny. I had breakfast in the saloon and during the morning sat on deck and read – or paced up and down. It was intensely boring all today – there was nothing to do. The ship was small – about 1200 tons – with very little accommodation in the way of smoking room and lounge *etc*. The cabins too were very small. It was a Norwegian boat. The passengers were Norwegian and English – about half in half. We had lunch in the saloon at 1.30. We were neither of us seasick all day. During most of the afternoon I lay down and slept or read, and occasionally paced the deck. Supper in the saloon at 8.0. I went to bed almost immediately afterwards.

Wednesday, October 1st, 1913

The ship reached Newcastle about 3 am. I got up at 7 am (= 6 English time, used henceforward) and Ludwig also soon afterwards. I found a customs official on board – and he passed our luggage through. He was the nicest douanier I have ever met – extremely apologetic and affable – passing everything and examining nothing! We came ashore with our luggage about 7.15 and drove in a taxi to the railway station. Thence we caught an 8 am train for London. We travelled 1st class. We had a large breakfast on the train soon after starting – and were very hungry for it! Later we went on with Ludwig's paper for the Working Men's College a lot. We also played dominoes. We had lunch on the train about 12.30. The train reached King's Cross station in London about 2.0. From the station we drove with our luggage in a taxi to the Grand Hotel, and there engaged two single rooms.

At the Grand Hotel Ludwig received a letter – which finally settled his scheme for exiling himself. That idea has been gradually crystallizing of late and he has talked about it a lot. When he first mentioned it I thought it absurd, but I have gradually got to think differently of it: he seems quite certain that, once settled and working well, he will be happy: and if he does good work out there, it will be just as good as any good work he might have done at Cambridge. At Cambridge – one might think – he could have done equally good work, but also further good work in teaching others: but he swears he can never do his best except in exile: and it is better to do good research and not teach – than to do indifferent research and also teach. The great difficulty about his particular kind of work is that – unless he absolutely settles all the foundations of Logic – his work will be of little value to the world. He has settled many difficulties, but there are still others unsolved. And it is probable that if he left a partial clearing up only of so abstract a subject – it would not carry conviction – it would not be clear (even so far as it went) – and it would perish with him. There is nothing between doing really great work and doing practically nothing. The news that arrived today in the letter, he had been expecting: it was that his sister and her husband were coming to live in London: he can't stand either of them:* and he won't live in England liable always to visits from them. So he is off to Norway in about 10 days! To a small village at the bottom of the Molde-fjord – about which he made enquiries at Bergen – where he will stay in a little inn and probably be quite alone. He goes to Cambridge tomorrow – to see Russell and others and to put his affairs in order there. He is coming to stay two nights at Lordswood after that – and then as soon as possible to Norway. It is all very wild and sudden – I can't imagine how things will work!

We had tea in the hotel about 4.30. Later we took a bus to Marble Arch and walked about in Hyde Park a bit. We came back by bus from Hyde Park Corner. At 7.30 we had dinner in the Grand Hotel Grill room. Later we went for a short stroll down by the embankment. Back to the Hotel and to bed by 10.0.

* He can't stand most of his family. His father – who died a year ago about – he was very fond of however. He has, I think, two sisters and two brothers alive. Two other brothers have committed suicide. His mother is still alive.

Thursday, October 2nd, 1913

Got up at 7.0 and had breakfast at 8.0. At 8.15 we left with our luggage in a taxi. I was put down at Euston and Ludwig went on to King's Cross and caught a 9 am train thence for Cambridge.

Monday, October 6th, 1913

After tea I went by bus down to New St station and met Ludwig, who is staying for two nights with us. He arrived, from Cambridge, at 6.2 pm and we drove up to Lordswood in a taxi. We had dinner at 7.15 as usual and afterwards talked and I played the piano a bit.

It seems that Russell and others at Cambridge, though much surprised by Ludwig's sudden Norway scheme, have made no objection and been in no way unpleasant about it: so he is off by boat to Bergen on Saturday next. He had very much dreaded talking to Russell about it – fearing that Russell might be unpleasant and think him a silly ass: but nothing of the sort seems to have happened. This evening he was pretty cheerful though rather restless: I think he is longing to get everything done and be settled down in Norway – he naturally does not altogether like parting with all his friends *etc* in England: these last few days will be somewhat disagreeable for him and he longs to get them over.

Tuesday, October 7th, 1913

After breakfast Ludwig and I went by bus down to town and did a lot of shopping – he bought sundry clothes for Norway. We came back with all his purchases in a taxi in time for lunch. After lunch I wrote a letter *etc* and Ludwig played on the player-piano. Several people called on Mother during the afternoon (after the party)*[21] but we§ escaped from them and had tea separately with Zelle and Hester and Richard. During the afternoon also Ludwig and I went down to the Post Office and he tried to telephone to the Whiteheads in London and arrange to see Dr Whitehead before he goes to Norway (the telephone at Lordswood seemed to be temporarily out of order – we could get no answer from the exchange – or we should have used it). He got through to the Whiteheads – but they were all out so it was no use. After tea we performed some Schubert in our usual way. At 5.30 Ludwig went off – by himself – to the Berlitz school in town – where we had arranged this morning for him to go and dictate a lot of his work in Logic to be typewritten (in German) for Russell.[22] He did not get back till after we had had our dinner – about 8.30. He had some dinner we had kept for him when he got in. Afterwards we sat and talked: he was quite cheerful and in very good form tonight.

* There are several such callers every afternoon for some time from now onwards.

§ Ludwig and I, and Zelle and Richard and Hester. Mother entertained them.

21 The Pinsents were moving to Oxford on Hume Pinsent's retirement, and gave two large parties before they left Birmingham.

22 The work referred to is known as *Notes on Logic*. The composition and histroy of these notes have caused some problems, eventually solved by Brian F. McGuinness in his paper 'Ludwig Wittgenstein's "Notes on Logic"', *Revue Internationale de Philosophie* 26, 1972.

Wednesday, October 8th, 1913

I got up at 6.15 to see Ludwig off. He had to go very early – back to Cambridge – as he has lots to do there. I saw him off from the house in a taxi at 7.0 – to catch a 7.30 am train from New St station. It was sad parting from him - but it is possible he may pay a short visit to England next summer (remaining in Norway till then and going back thither afterwards) when I may see him again. Our acquaintance has been chaotic but I have been very thankful for it: I am sure he has also. On the whole I enjoyed our Norway holiday very much and I know he did – as he says it is the best he has ever had.*...

It may as well be mentioned here what our expenses were in Norway. Ludwig paid for both of us and they amounted to about £80 altogether for the two of us.

* I am sure he does not feel about Norway as he felt about the Iceland holiday – or about me as he felt then – that he 'had enjoyed it as much as two people could who were nothing to each other'.

1914

Saturday, March 7th, 1914

I got a letter today from Ludwig in Norway. We have been corresponding, by the way, ever since we last parted. Ludwig has settled down in a small Inn at Skjolden on the Sognefjord, and except for a flying visit to Vienna last Xmas, which it appears he had to make very much against his will, has been there ever since October last. He seems to be tolerating life quite well – and the solitary exile seems to be suiting him. I hear from him that his work in Logic is progressing well. He is at present making arrangements to build himself a small house there – which is to be finished about next Autumn – so he must intend living there pretty permanently. But he intends coming back to England for about 2 months during this summer and in his letter to me today he suggests my going travelling with him again – 'to the Republic of Andorra (in the Pyrenees) or some such place'. I am very undecided whether to accept or not – and shall talk it over with Father and Mother before letting him know definitely. Last September, when he was so terribly difficult to get on with, I remember swearing to myself that never again would I go on a holiday alone with him. And if I went with him this Summer it would mean sacrificing the whole of my Summer holiday to it. Nevertheless it would be immensely interesting to go to Andorra. He says nothing about paying my expenses this time (as he has done in Iceland and Norway) – but I certainly couldn't afford to pay for myself at his scale of living. On the whole I expect I shall accept his proposal: at any rate I should like very much to see him again.

Tuesday, March 24th, 1914

I have decided to go with Ludwig, travelling, this summer – to Andorra or some such place. I wrote to him today saying I could come with him for about 2 to 3 weeks. I expect I shall have a little longer holiday than that as a matter of fact – but I want to spend a little time at Oxford with Mother and Father.

Wednesday, April 29th, 1914

After supper I played the piano and later wrote out some research I have just begun on the question 'What is Truth'. The ideas came to me in the course of a conversation with Adam[1] and Thomson the other day and lately I have been thinking a good deal on the question and begun to put it all on paper. The result – if correct – is amazing. I seem to have answered Pilate's question – and incidentally to have settled the Theory of types difficulty as well. (By the way about a month ago Ludwig wrote to me that he had settled Types and in fact put the whole of Logic in order and was writing a book on the subject – but the general question of Truth is not exactly part of Logic). Of course I can't really say yet how good my research is. I shall have to consider it

[1] N. K. Adam (d. 1973), undergraduate, 1911–14, a Fellow, 1915–23, of Trinity College. He was Professor of Chemistry at Southampton University, 1937–57.

and digest it some time before I can feel at all confident. Then, if I do, I might possibly send it to Russell – together with another little bit of research on the logical nature of Probability, I did some time ago – which still seems to me to settle that too.[2]

David Pinsent stopped writing his diary in the summer of 1914. The remaining extracts are from two 'supplements' written in the autumn after the war had broken out.

July 1914

In the middle of the week I wrote to Wittgenstein in Vienna, for he had lately returned thither from Norway, about our intended holiday together during late August and early September:[3] there was some question still exactly where we should go, and as we hadn't much time the question of going somewhere near afield, and not to a far off place like Spain, had been suggested: and I remember I wrote suggesting Scotland but dissuading Ireland in view of the possibility of civil war there.

August – September 1914[4]

In the course of August and September I got two letters from Wittgenstein and I got a third just recently about the end of November. The first was from Vienna dated about

[2] The Manuscripts of Pinsent's papers on truth and on probability no longer exist. It is not known whether Russell ever saw them. See also below, DP to LW, 22 August 1916.

[3] See below DP to LW, 22 and 29 July 1914.

[4] This entry, although headed 'August–September', must have been written early in December.

August 2nd, the second from Krakau dated August 11th, and the third, also from Krakau, dated November 11th. The first two arrived direct from Austria to England, addressed to me from Austria direct, but the third was sent via the 'Comité International de la Croix-Rouge, Geneva, Switzerland' and forwarded by them. Ludwig was caught in Austria when war broke out and not allowed to leave: he began by doing voluntary civilian work[5] in connection with the war, but in his second letter he said he had joined the Army. He was not liable to compulsory military service – on medical grounds – but enlisted voluntarily. He appears to be in the Artillery and quartered at Krakau. I think it is magnificent of him to have enlisted – but extremely sad and tragic. In his last letter he says he has done a lot of work at Logic since the war began – so I suppose his military duties don't take up all his time. He writes praying we may meet again some day. Poor fellow – I hope to God we shall. I have written three letters to him in answer to his, two via Cecil[6] in Florence and the last via the 'Comité international de la Croix Rouge'.[7] I don't know however whether any of them have reached him. Of course we can't say much, as our letters are all censored.

[5] Nothing more is known about this. On 7 August 1914 Wittgenstein enlisted as a volunteer in the army. He served to the end of the war, when he was taken prisoner.

[6] Cecil Pinsent, a cousin of David Pinsent, was working as an architect on Bernard Berenson's villa I Tatti near Florence.

[7] The first two letters have not been found. Quite probably they failed to reach Wittgenstein. The third is the letter below, dated 1 December 1914.

Letters
1914–1919

David Pinsent to Wittgenstein

105 Harborne Road,
Edgbaston,
Wednesday Birmingham

My dear Ludwig,

Thanks very much for your letter. Then I may hope to see you in Birmingham about August 13th. Let me know exactly when you will appear.

G'Log. is quoted as follows:
'$6\frac{7}{8}$–$7\frac{1}{32}$ ex. div.' and if you don't understand that, I shall be delighted to give you a long lecture on the custom and usage of the Stock Exchange when you come to Birmingham!

How goes G'Log.?
Ever yours
David H. G'Pymph

Wednesday – This note has no other date, nor is it signed. It is presumably the first in the sequence of letters which follows. Pinsent was at that time lodging with a family friend, Miss Dale, and working in his father's firm, Pinsent & Co., while reading Law. His parents had moved to Foxcombe Hill, near Oxford.
G'Log – I have not been able to provide an explanation of this sign, nor of the meaning of the signature *G'Pymph* in this and the following letter.

David Pinsent to Wittgenstein

105 Harborne Road,
Edgbaston,
Tuesday, July 7th [1914] Birmingham

My dear Ludwig,

Thanks so very much for your letter. On week-days, except Saturday, I am always free after about 5.30 pm for the rest of the evening. On Saturdays I am free after about 12 noon for the rest of the day. On Sundays I am free all day. The best thing, I think, would be for us to meet for some week-end – say at Cambridge (I suppose you will be going there probably). It would be very nice indeed if you came to Birmingham – so long as you wouldn't be bored to have nothing to do all the time I was at that Bloody G'off.

I suggest that you should put a brass plate on the door of your house

'G'LOG LIMITED
REGISTERED OFFICE'

inscribed thereon.

There isn't much to say – except that G'Log is pretty high.

Ever yours,
David H. G'Pymph

Bloody G'off – Presumably the offices of Pinsent & Co.
your house – Presumably the hut which Wittgenstein had decided to have built for himself at Skjolden in Norway.

David Pinsent to Wittgenstein

105 Harborne Road,
Edgbaston,
Birmingham

July 22nd 1914

My dear Ludwig,

Thanks for your letter. It will suit me just as well to start on August the 25th – returning about September 15th. I will assume then, unless I hear to the contrary from you, that we start on the 25th Aug. Let me know where and when to meet you.

Ever yours –
G'Dave

start on the 25th Aug – Refers to the journey which Pinsent and Wittgenstein were planning to 'Andorra or some such place' in the late summer of 1914. See diary, entry of 7 March 1914, and the next letter.

David Pinsent to Wittgenstein

Please address your next letter thus → Glenfield, Foxcombe Hill, Near Oxford

Wednesday, July 19th [1914]

My dear Ludwig,

Very many thanks for your letter. I will meet you in London then on the 24th August. I will be at the Grand Hotel – Trafalgar Square – from about 5 pm onwards at that afternoon unless I hear to the contrary from you.

About where we are to go – I don't know how long it takes to get to Andorra – but is it longer than it takes to get to the Faeroe islands? Do you think there would be anywhere where we could stay in the Faeroe islands – there are not likely to be any inns and I don't know if we could be certain of finding any house where they would put us up. It would be rather fun to go there however if it could be managed.

I suppose Madeira wouldn't suit you: you can get there in 4 days from Southampton – by the Union Castle Line of steamers – but that means starting from Southampton on a Saturday evening which would have to be August the 22nd. I don't know if you could manage that. We shouldn't stay at Funchal – which is crowded with Tourists – but we might cross the island to a place called Santa Anna – which I have visited – where there is a tiny but quite comfortable inn – and very few tourists. People occasionally go there but hardly any. It is a most beautiful country and I personally should love to revisit it. If we went there – it would be as well to get tickets early.

Of course there are out of the way places in the British Isles: I don't think we had better go to Ireland, as there will almost certainly be riots and civil war of a sort there soon! – but Scotland – say the Orkney, Shetland, or Hebrides Islands might do. Perhaps – in view of this European War business we had better not go to Andorra – it might be difficult to get back.

Ever yours
G'Dave

which I have visited – See above, diary entry for 30 August 1913 and fn 14.

David Pinsent to Wittgenstein

Glenfield,
Foxcombe Hill,
Near Oxford

December 1st 1914

My dear Ludwig,

I was awfully glad to get your letter, sent *via* Switzerland. I have received three letters – including that one – since the War began – from you. I have sent two letters to you since about September 1st last – both *via* a cousin of mine who lives in Italy. I know they were forwarded from Italy, so I hope very much you will have received them.

I was in Cambridge about a month ago for two nights and I saw Russell and also Hardy – who both asked after you. I told them what I knew of you and that you had joined the Army as a volunteer.

I tried to join the Army here, but I am not up to the medical standard for a Private (I am too thin) and I couldn't get a Commission as an officer. So I am going on as usual as a civilian, reading Law.

I think of you very often and do hope all is well with you. When this war is over we will meet each other again. Let's hope it will be soon!

I am sending this via Switzerland.

Au Revoir and God bless you! Ever
yours
G'Dave

I am so glad you have done Mathematical work lately. I wish you were here and we could talk about G'Log again!

I think it was *splendid* of you to volunteer for the Army – though it is horribly tragic that it should be necessary.

I have received three letters – See above diary entry for August–September 1914 and fn 6.
Hardy – G. H. Hardy (1877–1947), the mathematician, was in 1914 Cayley lecturer in mathematics at Cambridge.

David Pinsent to Wittgenstein

Glenfield,
Foxcombe Hill,
Nr Oxford

January 14th, 1915

My dear Ludwig,

Thanks so very much for your letter – dated the 4th January 1915 – which I have just received. Your letters to me seem to go much quicker than mine to you: at any rate I am so glad you have got one of mine at last – the one dated 30th August. There are two others, besides this one and the one you have got, which ought sometime to reach you both addressed to Krakau. I have together received four letters from you (including the one just arrived) since the War began.

I very often think of you and wonder how you are getting on. There is very little to say – except that I hope to God we shall see each other again after the War.

God bless you! Ever yours –
G'Dave

David Pinsent to Wittgenstein

Glenfield,
Foxcombe Hill,
Nr Oxford

Wednesday, January 27th, 1915

My dear Ludwig

Your letter, dated December 20th or thereabouts, reached me a day or two later than the one dated Jan. 4th.

The Red Cross Switzerland seems the only sure way of sending letters.

I have written to Moore at Cambridge and sent him your message *etc*. I thought I had better write as it is unlikely that I shall be able to go to Cambridge myself again soon. I also told him, in my letter to him, how to get a letter through to you – so I hope he will write to you.

I am working away at the G'Law – but now mostly in London. I spend a lot of time in the Courts now – listening to cases.

There isn't much to say – but that I hope very much indeed that we shall see each other again soon, after the War.

Ever yours –
G'Dave

I am working – Pinsent was working for his uncle Robert Parker, Judge of the High Court. See next letter.

David Pinsent to Wittgenstein

Glenfield,
Foxcombe Hill,
March 2nd 1915 Nr Oxford

My dear Ludwig,

Thanks awfully for your letter – dated February 10th – which I have just received. I *have* sent all my recent letters to you *via* the 'Agence du Croix Rouge des prisonniers de guerre – Genève', but even so they seem very variable in the time they take – sometimes 10 days and sometimes over 3 weeks.

I have not been able to go to Cambridge lately I am afraid. I have not heard of Russell's new book, but will try to find out about it and if possible send it to you. I wrote to Moore and sent him your messages. Have you heard from him? I hoped he might perhaps write to you and I told him how best to get letters through to you.

I have been writing a paper on Philosophy. I am not at

present taking it very seriously and dreaming of publishing it or anything like that, as it is probably absolutely rot! It is not so much about the details of Logic, as about what Logic as a whole is *about* and what 'Truth' is and 'Knowledge'. The whole business seems very clear to me as a matter of fact, But I dare say what seems clear to me is all rot! I wish you were here and could talk it over with me!

I am exceedingly busy these days with Law *etc.* I am a sort of private secretary to my uncle, who is a Judge, and my work occupies me pretty well all day during 5 days in each week. I live in London most of the week, though I go to Oxford for the week ends.

I wish to God this horrible tragedy would end, and I am longing to see you again.

Ever your friend,
David

letter – dated February 10th – The beginning of a draft (*Entwurf*) of this letter has been preserved. It goes as follows:

My *dear* Davy,
Got today your letter dated January 27th. This is about the limit. I'm now beginning to be more fertile again

Russell's new book – Presumably *Our Knowledge of the External World.* Wittgenstein had had news about its appearance from J. M. Keynes and wanted if possible to obtain a copy of it. For all we know his wish remained unfulfilled. See Ludwig Wittgenstein, *Briefe*, herausgegeben von B. F. McGuinness und G. H. von Wright (Frankfurt am Main: Suhrkamp Verlag, 1980).

David Pinsent to Wittgenstein

Glenfield,
Foxcombe Hill,
Near Oxford

April 6th, 1915

My dear Ludwig,
Thank you so much for your letter, dated March 18th. I am so sorry if Moore won't behave like a Christian: as a matter of fact he never acknowledged my letter.

My paper on philosophy has expanded to some length, and now purports to say what Ethics and Philosophy in general are *about* as well as Logic: also what 'truth' is – there seem to be at least seven sorts of truth. I should very much like to send you a copy of it and to know what you think of it – but all our letters seem to have to pass the Censor, and I fancy the Censor might object to having to read through 50 type-written pages of Philosophy in search of any information which might be of value to the enemy!

I think of you very often and wonder what you are doing. I am having three weeks holiday just now, but I begin work again in London after that.

Ever your friend,
Davy

Moore won't behave like a Christian. – Wittgenstein and Moore had had a quarrel before the war, after Moore's visit to Wittgenstein in Norway in April 1914. In July Wittgenstein wrote to Moore a letter of reconciliation. Moore, who had reason to be offended, did not reply nor did he evidently react to the greetings sent to him through Pinsent. See *Briefe*, Nr 46 and comments. See also the reference to an extract from Moore's diary of 1915 in the picture biography *Wittgenstein, sein Leben in Bildern und Texten.* Herausgegeben von Michael Nedo und Michele Ranchetti (Frankfurt am Main: Suhrkamp Verlag, 1983, p. 141).

David Pinsent to Wittgenstein

Glenfield,
Foxcombe Hill,
Nr Oxford

28th June 1915

My dear Ludwig,

Thanks awfully for your letter dated 2nd June. I am afraid a letter of mine must have gone astray.

I was up for a week end at Cambridge the other day, but very few people were there. I called at Russell's but he was out.

I am still working very very hard, and am getting rather

sick of the Law. I go for long walks in the country most week ends, which is rather nice.

I am afraid there is nothing to say. I should love to talk about the work you have been doing in Logic.

I heard Beethoven's fifth and seventh Symphonies and Schubert's Unfinished at a single concert the other day. And about 3 months ago quite a lot of Beethoven and Brahms, including the 9th Symphony and the Requiem and the Missa Solemnis. I wish you had been with me!

Lets hope we shall meet again some time.

Ever your friend,
David

David Pinsent to Wittgenstein

Glenfield,
Foxcombe Hill,
2 of Sept. 1915 Near Oxford

My dear Ludwig,

Thank you so much for your letter dated July 10th. I am so sorry about your nervous shock – still it must be nice to get a short furlough.

I have given up the study of that damned Law – for the present at any rate – I am now on Government work – working very long hours.

We have the 'Promenade concerts' on now in London. I have been to one – but I have very little spare time. I heard Beethoven's 2nd Symphony at that one – also a magnificent Piano Concerto of Brahms!

I often think of you and wonder what you are doing.

Ever your friend,
David

nervous shock – There had been a heavy explosion in the artillery workshop in Kracow where Wittgenstein was working. Wittgenstein suffered a nervous shock and also some physical damage and was for some time afterwards in hospital. If Wittgenstein's letter to Pinsent was dated July 10th, the time of the explosion as indicated in a letter from Wittgenstein to Ludwig von Ficker of late July 1915 cannot be correct. Cf *Briefe*, Nr 74.

David Pinsent to Wittgenstein

(31st May 1916)

My dear Ludwig,

Many thanks for your letter which I received today. I am very sorry indeed that my letters haven't reached you. I sent them through an agency in Switzerland, but this one I send through the same lady through whom I have received your letters; so it is certain that this one will reach you. My earlier letters, although not written long ago, have evidently gone astray, because you ought to have received many in the last 6 months. It grieves me infinitely and I can only hope that you will get this communication and that it will explain everything to you. – My dear Ludwig, I feel so very sorry for you, when I hear from you, that you have recently had to live through difficult times. Bear them with courage, and after the war we shall no doubt at once do our very best to see each other again. Believe me, I miss you very much! Imagine, my brother Richard, who went out to France in the war, was killed in France a couple of months ago. He and you were the two persons whom I most of all liked to see and wanted to be with – and now he is no longer there. Now I long even more to see you again. The War cannot change our personal relations; it has really nothing to do with personal relationships. I assure you that it has not in the least influenced my feelings towards you. For a second time some 5 months ago I was refused service in the army for medical reasons, and work at present extremely hard in connection with the war as – incredible to me – a mechanic. I have not heard much music lately, I am sorry to say. – Please, write to me again when you have received this and tell me how you are – that all goes well with you. I look forward confidently to seeing you again and we shall both wait patiently for that moment. It *will* come, and it will be splendid after so long to go back to the times we had together and which, like so many other things, now appear so distant and almost inconceivable.

Ever your friend,
Davy

This letter exists in typescript only. (All the others are handwritten.) It is in German, evidently translated from an original in English. The German letter is headed '*Abschrift 1*' (Copy 1.) Under this it reads 'Wien I., Albrechtgasse 3' and under this 'Küsnacht (Zch), Gut Wangensbach, 31. Mai 16'. At the end is the address 'Hochwohlgeborenen Herrn Ludwig Wittgenstein, K.u.k. Feldhaubitzenreg. Nr. 5, IV. Batterie, Feldpost Nr. 189'. On the sheets there are some jottings in Wittgenstein's hand – not, however, connected with the content of the letter.
The date when the letter actually was composed is not clear. The date 31st May is presumably that on which the German translation was forwarded from Switzerland. David Pinsent's brother Richard was killed in the war in October 1915. The letter says 'a couple of months ago' ('vor 1 oder 2 Monaten'). This would indicate that it was written at the end of 1915 or in the beginning of 1916. But it also says that 'some 5 months ago' Pinsent was for a second time refused service. This happened in the beginning of 1916. In March he began working 'as a mechanic'. (See the Introduction by Anne Keynes, above p. xvi.) In all probability, therefore, the letter was actually written in May 1916.
through the same lady – Frau Elsa Gröger. See *Briefe*, Nr. 75.
difficult times – In the first half of 1916 Wittgenstein was for several months continuously in the fighting line. In July he was then sent to a Reserve Officers' School in Olmütz in Moravia. For details, see Brian McGuinness *Wittgenstein, A Life* ch. 7, especially pp. 237ff.

David Pinsent to Wittgenstein

22nd August 1916

My dear Ludwig,

Thank you very much for your letter of 31st July which I got today. I am so glad that everything is still good with you. I think it admirable that you still have time and energy to think about the old philosophical problems. Until about eight months ago I too did the same. I also wrote a longish

Essay which you must see one day, but latterly I had to work so hard that I no longer had time for that. – I am an engineer or rather a craftsman; I work in a factory for engines. It is very interesting but also very fatiguing. For many months I have had no holidays except for 5 days sick leave recently when I went out sailing in a small boat. – It is a long time since I visited Cambridge and it is difficult for me to go there, but I shall write to Russell and give him greetings from you and tell him that he can write to you. – I long to see you again; as soon as the War is over we shall meet, if necessary – in Switzerland.

Ever your friend,
Davy

P.S. My mother asks me especially to tell you that she very much hopes to see you in our home in England when the War is over, and she thanks you most sincerely for your condolences on the occasion of Richard's death.

Ever yours
Davy

This letter too, and the following one, is in German. Both are in handwriting, but the script is not Pinsent's.

Essay – The German word is 'Abhandlung'. The typescript of an essay by Pinsent with the title 'Philosophy' still exists. The main part of it was written during February and March 1915. There are four appendices to it, written between May 1915 and March 1916. The whole typescript has sixty pages in all.

sickleave – Pinsent spent a few days sickleave with his parents and sister at the Radfords' cottage in Cornwall in August, sailing several times in Falmouth Harbour.

David Pinsent to Wittgenstein

14th September 1916

My dear Ludwig,

I have just heard from Russell and he asks me to give you his very best regards and wishes and to congratulate you that you also in spite of present conditions have made progress with your philosophical work. He says he wrote to you some time ago but did not receive any answer and was worried about you; but he assumes that his letter never reached you. – I often think of you and ask myself how you are getting on. I hope that all goes well with you, I myself am still working hard. Recently I played the accompaniment (Schubert) for a friend who sings. Something from the old 'Wintertag' which we used to play.

Please God that we shall soon be able to play again!

Ever your friend,

Davy

his letter never reached you – Russell had written to Wittgenstein at the end of November 1915. Wittgenstein got the letter but whether he replied to it we do not know. No trace of their correspondence between November 1916 and February 1919 remains.

'Wintertag' – presumably 'Winterreise' by Schubert. At the bottom of the sheet there is a logical formula written in Frege's symbolism. It is here reproduced from the original

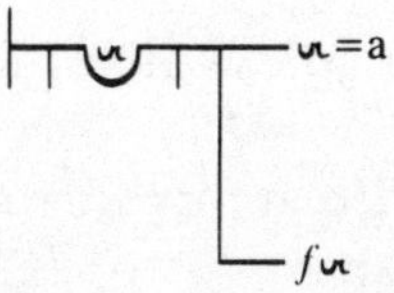

$\mathfrak{a} = a$

$f\mathfrak{a}$

The formula says that there exists a thing such that if this thing is (has the property) *f*, then it is identical with (the thing) *a*.

Ellen F. Pinsent to Wittgenstein

Little Wick,
Selly Hill,
Nr Birmingham

6th July 1918

My dear Mr Wittgenstein,

I know you will be very grieved to hear the sad news I have to tell you. My son David was killed while flying on the 8th May. He was engaged in research on Aerodynamics and he had done a great deal of very valuable work. He was perfectly happy when flying, he loved it, and I think during the last months of his life he was as happy as a man could be. He had found the work for which he was really fitted and felt himself of real use. We are told that the work he did will be the means of saving many lives in the future and he met his death investigating the cause of a previous accident.

I want to tell you how much he loved you and valued your friendship up to the last. I saw him the day before he was killed and we talked of you. He spoke of you always with great affection and regretted that he could not write to you. He was afraid that the few letters he was able to write earlier in the war may not have reached you. He has had some letters from you, but I expect not all, and latterly he believed that nothing he wrote would reach you. We often talked of you and hoped to see you as soon as the War is over.

Mr Pinsent and I hope that you will find us out directly Peace comes for we want to tell you all about David and to assure you of his constant love and friendship. Hester too sends you messages and hopes to see you again. I am keeping you some books of David's which I know he would like you to have.

You will know how great our sorrow is for you know what a greathearted son we have lost. We do not want to lose his friends, therefore let us meet as soon as we can. I think I should get a letter if you answer this.

Little Wick – The Pinsents returned to Birmingham during the war so that Hume Pinsent could take his nephews' place in the office, two of whom had been killed.

Wittgenstein to Ellen F. Pinsent

Most honoured, dear, gracious Lady,

Today I received your kind letter with the sad news of David's death. David was my first and my only friend. I have indeed known many young men of my own age and have been on good terms with some, but only in him did I find a real friend, the hours I have spent with him have been the best in my life, he was to me a brother and a friend. Daily I have thought of him and have longed to see him again. God will bless him. If I live to see the end of the war I will come and see you and we will talk of David.

One more thing, I have just finished the philosophic work on which I was already at work at Cambridge. I had always hoped to be able to show it to him sometime, and it will always be connected with him in my mind. I will dedicate it to David's memory. For he always took great interest in it, and it is to him I owe far the most part of the happy moods which made it possible for me to work. Will you please say to Mr Pinsent and to Miss Hester how very deeply I sympathise with them in their loss. I shall never forget the dear one so long as I live, nor shall I forget you who were nearest to him.

Yours true and thankful
L. W.

This letter, and the one of 24th March 1919, from Wittgenstein to Mrs Pinsent was written in German and later translated into English. The German originals no longer exist.
the sad news – We do not know exactly when Wittgenstein received the news of David Pinsent's death. The dedication to Pinsent appears on a separate page already in the manuscript known as the *Prototractatus*. When this was written and finished is not known with certainty. The final version of the book was probably a typescript which Wittgenstein dictated before going to the Italian front at the end of September 1918.

Ellen F. Pinsent to Ludwig Wittgenstein

Little Wick,
Selly Hill,
Nr Birmingham

Dec. 24th 1918

My dear Ludwig,

I am wondering so much how you are getting on for I fear you may be having a very dreadful time till things become more quiet and settled. We are all so glad to think this War is over and I hope it may soon be possible for you to return to England when we shall hope so much to see you.

I was so glad to get your letter and to hear all you said about David – and we are proud to think that your book is to be dedicated to him. I am sure that would have pleased him very greatly. He so often used to talk to me of you and of your work. I like to think that you will come some day and that we shall talk of him together.

I wish I knew that you were well and happy. There ought not to be any difficulty now about letters so do write and tell me how you are and what you are doing? and all about yourself and your hopes for the future, for your happiness and welfare are very dear to me. You see I have called you Ludwig because David always spoke of you to me as Ludwig.

Our love and good wishes to you for Christmas and the New Year. Always your affec[tion] ate friend,

Ellen F. Pinsent

Wittgenstein to Ellen F. Pinsent

24. 3. 1919

Honoured, loved, gracious Lady,

Only the day before yesterday did I receive, to my great joy, your letter of the 24 Dec. 1918. Since the beginning of November I have been a prisoner of war. I am getting on all right. Ordinarily I can write postcards, this letter I am sending by an officer who is returning home. What I shall do when I get home I do not yet know myself. But at any rate I shall try to meet my friends again as soon as it is possible. My book will be published as soon as I get home. It is true that the meeting to which I most looked forward during these five years has not been allowed to me. Nearly every day I think of dear David. May things go well with you always.

With heartiest greetings to you from your truly grateful L. W. My address is Cassino, Italia, Campo concentramento, Prigionieri Guerra, Reparto Ufficiali.

Ellen F. Pinsent to Wittgenstein

Foxcombe Hill,
Nr Oxford

May 9th 1919

My dear Ludwig,

I was so *very* glad to hear from you – but oh I am so sorry that you are a prisoner. I do hope that it will not be long now before you are released and that you will get something of real interest to do. It must be so hard for a man of your intellect to remain a prisoner cut off from all work. I am so glad you had finished your book.

I have a letter and a postcard to thank you for – dated 24th April – the letter reached me the soonest. Fancy my letter of December taking all that time to reach you! Well, it is something to feel that Peace is within sight and after it comes, I hope we shall all love one another. I feel that we shall all have learned a great deal and I am hopeful that we shall all work together for mankind.

It is just a year since David died and I seem to long for him back again more than ever – but I do not weep over it. I am proud of the work he did and the brave death he died – and I know how you loved him and I shall always love you. Come to us as soon as ever you can and you will find a warm welcome. There are some things of David's I want you to have.

We have at last been able to get home and the address at the top of this letter is my permanent one and will always find me. Please let me know your address when you get home – and do write again soon. We all send you love and remembrances.

Yours always aftec[tion]ately,
Ellen F. Pinsent

POSTSCRIPTUM

In a letter of June 1922 from Wittgenstein to C. K. Ogden, Wittgenstein asks for Mrs Pinsent's address (she had moved from Oxford to London after her husband's death in 1920) and says that he must send her a copy of the *Tractatus* which was then about to appear. The request is repeated in a letter of July. Ogden sent the book to Mrs Pinsent and she thanked Ogden for it (letter 20.11.1922) and said she was going to write to Wittgenstein. Her letter to Wittgenstein, however, is not known to exist. The above information is recorded in Ludwig Wittgenstein, *Letters to C. K. Ogden with Comments on the English Translation of the Tractatus Logico-Philosophicus*, Edited with an Introduction by G. H. von Wright (Oxford/London: Basil Blackwell/Routledge & Kegan Paul, 1973).

Bibliography

Coffey, P. *The Science of Logic*, London: Longmans, Green and Co., 1912.

McGuinness, Brian F. 'Ludwig Wittgenstein's "Notes on Logic"', *Revue Internationale de Philosophie* 26, 1972.

—— *Wittgenstein, A Life: Young Ludwig* (1889–1921), London: Gerald Duckworth and Co. Ltd, 1988.

—— and von Wright, G. H. von eds, *Briefe*, Frankfurt am Main: Suhrkamp Verlag, 1980.

Moore, G. E. *Principia Ethica*, Cambridge: Cambridge University Press, 1903.

Nedo, Michael and Ranchetti, Michele eds, *Wittgenstein, sein Leben in Bildern und Texten* (Frankfurt am Main: Suhrkamp Verlag, 1983).

Russell, Bertrand *Our Knowledge of the External World*, The Open Court Publishing Company, 1914.

Wittgenstein, Ludwig Briefe, ed. Brian F. McGuinness and G. H. von Wright, Frankfurt am Main: Suhrkamp Verlag, 1980.

—— *Notes on Logic*, in *Ludwig Wittgenstein, Notebooks 1914–1916*, 2nd ed., Oxford: Basil Blackwell, 1979.

—— review of P. Coffey, *The Science of Logic* (1912), in *Cambridge Review* 34, 6 March 1913, p. 351.

Index